David Blackburn

David Blackburn *and the* Visionary Landscape Tradition

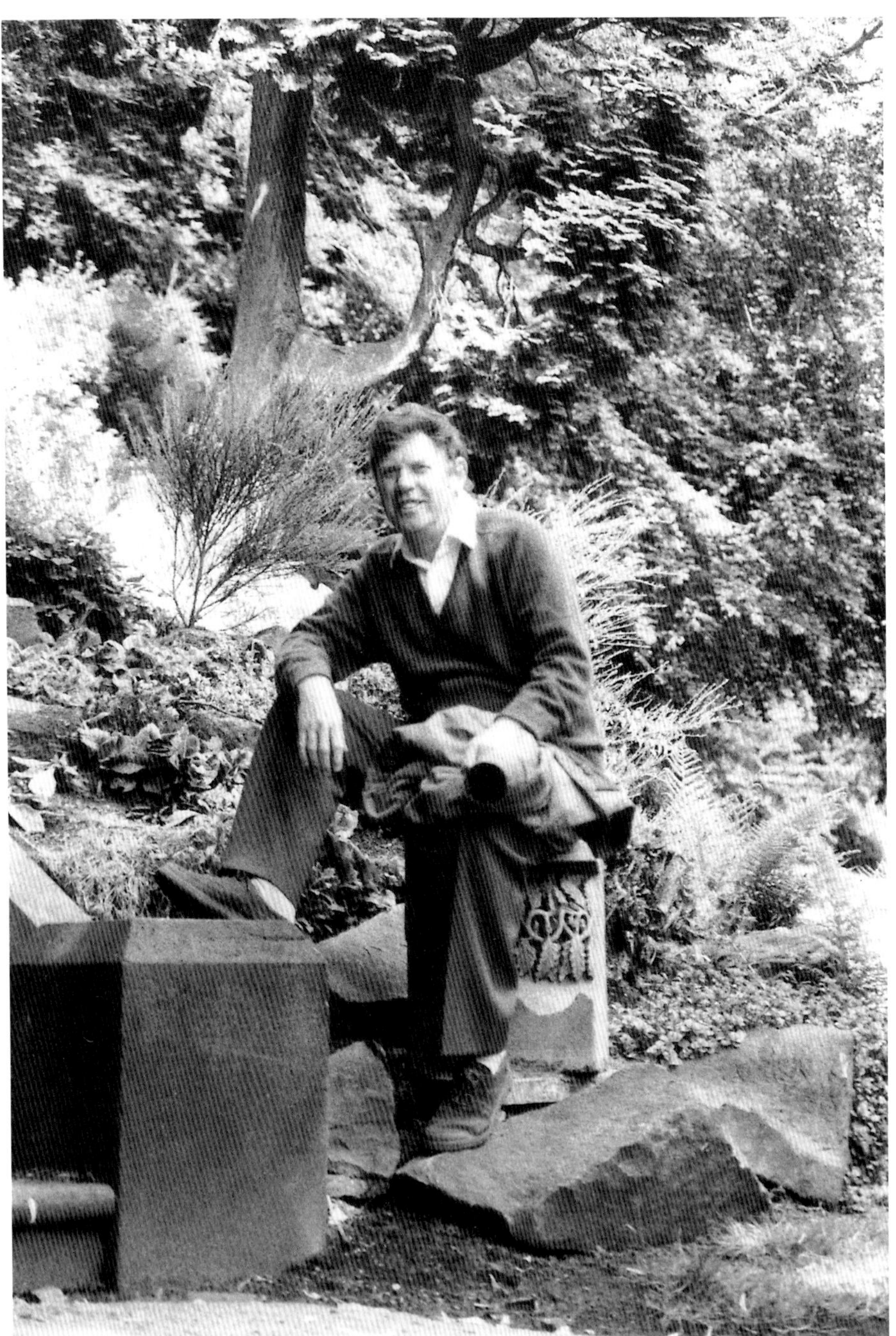

David Blackburn

DAVID BLACKBURN
and the
VISIONARY LANDSCAPE TRADITION

SASHA GRISHIN

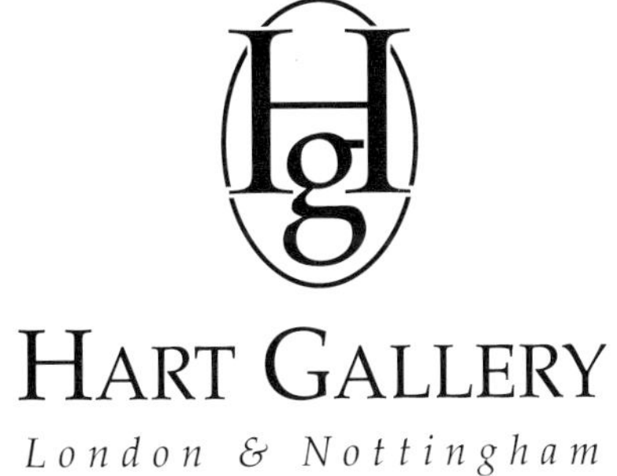

HART GALLERY
London & Nottingham

Cover: Two Stones and Hillside – Evening, 1990
Pastel
16" × 13 1/2"

ISBN: 0 9520759-2-X

Colour Photographs by: Richard Littlewood

Designed and Printed by: Jones & Palmer Ltd. 021-236 9007

DEDICATED TO NATASHA GRISHIN

Acknowledgements

This book was first discussed in 1977 after I had known David Blackburn for about a decade and he had come to Canberra on one of his frequent journeys to Australia. A second, more or less serious attempt at a book was made in 1984, when David was once more in Canberra and further interviews were recorded. And so the situation may have continued if it had not been for the energetic intervention of John Hart who simply disregarded excuses concerning pressure of work and logistics, set a firm timetable with inflexible deadlines and, with the single-mindedness of a mountaineer, power steered this project to fruition.

A book which has grown so slowly over so many years has incurred many debts along the way, too many to accurately remember and fully acknowledge. Naturally, more than anyone else I need to thank the artist who for over a quarter of a century has been generous with his time, forgiving and outstanding in his patience. Professor Joseph Burke who first introduced me to the artist has been inspirational and I acknowledge my debt to Lord Clark, Humphrey Brooke, Patrick White and Patrick McCaughey. Lady Margaret Kagan in Boston and Lord Joseph Kagan in London have been of enormous support during a number of difficult times. Numerous people in Huddersfield have gone out of their way to help in the research, show their collections and to share in their knowledge of David Blackburn. Richard Littlewood I thank sincerely for doing most of the photography for this book. The involvement of Kirklees Metropolitan Council has been invaluable. John and Katherine Hart have intervened at many crucial stages when things seemed ready to fall apart and without their support, friendship and enthusiasm, the project would have floundered.

Natasha Grishin supported me over many difficulties and brought sunshine to a Yorkshire winter. It is to her that this book is dedicated.

CONTENTS

DAVID BLACKBURN AND THE VISIONARY LANDSCAPE TRADITION

Most of David Blackburn's work over the past few decades deals with landscapes. However, the primary concern is not with the literal transcription of a landscape of observable facts, nor even with the landscape which represents a state of mind, but with a landscape which serves the role of a visual metaphor, a visionary landscape which on earth provides a glimpse of paradise.

In a famous letter, the twenty-three year old Samuel Palmer noted that "the general characteristics of Nature's beauty not only differ from, but are, in some respects, opposed to those of Imaginative Art" and "We find hundreds in rapture when they get into the fields, who have not the least relish for grand art . . . [as] Nature does not leave a space for the soul to climb above her steepest summits" and it is creation which "sometimes pours into the spiritual eye the radiance of Heaven".[1] For Samuel Palmer "Terrestrial Spring showers blossoms and odours in profusion, which at some moments 'Breathe on earth the air of Paradise': indeed sometimes, when the spirits are in Heav'n, earth itself, as in emulation, blooms into Eden."[2] Palmer in his early visionary landscapes, which owe as much to the

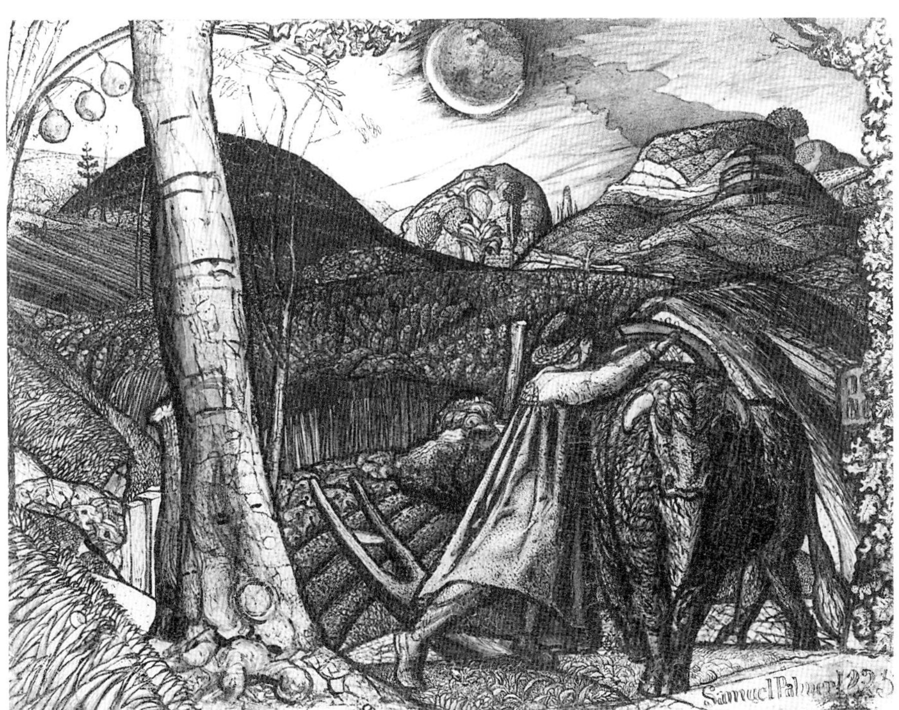

Samuel Palmer A Rustic Scene, 1825
Pen & Brown Ink
179mm × 236mm
© Ashmolean Museum, Oxford

topography of Shoreham in Kent as to the liberating imagination of William Blake, transformed the physical reality of a specific landscape into a celestial vision. In the landscape he saw a veil of heaven through which the artist strove to catch a glimpse of Eden.

Although largely unrecognised by his contemporaries, the youthful work of Palmer has been rehabilitated in the twentieth century as "an outpouring of the unfettered Romantic imagination".[3] Within the prevailing Francophile linear construct of modern Western European art history, where the centre of art is seen as being exclusively in Paris and developments outside of France are considered as insignificant, Palmer has been regarded as a minor Romantic mystic whose artistic experience was valid for a very short period of time, before being swept aside by the mid-century tide of realist painting. When, a century later, Graham Sutherland in the 1920s turned to the early works of Palmer as an inspiration, even to his admirers this was an aberration. Apologetically the work was dismissed as "unmistakably Palmerish, that is to say picturesque, pastoral, weather-conscious, rather sentimental, and a little too full of 'the felicity of Olde England'".[4] For Sutherland, Palmer was the tranquil visionary who was a great liberating force that legitimised a rejection of mainstream Parisian modernism and the prevailing fashion for the cubist restructuring of space. In 1961 Douglas Cooper observed that "To this day, Sutherland approaches his subjects head-on and does not try to see around them, nor to twist them in order to show other sides, means by which cubist painters succeeded in evoking volume and recession in a shallow pictorial space. For all the modernism of his idiom and the pictorial liberties which he has been prepared to take, Sutherland is in this sense a traditionalist."[5]

More recently there has been an attempt made to offer an alternative interpretation to the development of modern Western European art, one which largely bypasses the developments in Paris altogether. Rather than primarily examining the formal devices used to establish and to redefine pictorial space, Robert Rosenblum advanced a coherent alternate reading of the history of modern art, a "counter-French tradition", which had a focus on the Northern European Romantic tradition where questions of intuitive spirituality and an essentially emotional and non-cerebral response to nature took precedence over purely formal values.[6] Within this tradition, mysticism and the romantic temperament were the constant factors. The author traced this tradition of art as an unbroken continuum from Friedrich and Blake, through van Gogh, Hodler, Munch, Kandinsky, Klee and Mondrian, and right through to the Abstract Expressionists like Gottlieb, Newman and Rothko. In this tradition of modern art a central place is occupied by the work of Palmer and Sutherland. It is to this tradition that the art of David Blackburn belongs.

In 1959, when David Blackburn turned twenty, a number of key decisions which were to determine his subsequent work had already taken place. That year he had completed his four years of study at the Huddersfield School of Art and he had secured a scholarship to the prestigious Royal College of Art in London, an exclusively postgraduate school of art and design which by then had started to challenge the supremacy of the Slade as England's leading art school. At the RCA he enrolled in Textiles in October 1959, while at the same time David Hockney, R.B. Kitaj, Derek Boshier, Allen Jones, Frank Bowling and Peter Phillips enrolled in the painting school. Many of them emerged as leading figures of the English Pop Art scene in the *Young Contemporaries* exhibitions of 1960–62. In the next three years, neither the RCA nor the great collections of art of the capital in which Blackburn spent much of his time, were to have a major impact on his thinking about art. From the outset he held a conviction that the purpose of art was to invest observable phenomena with transcendental significance. Art was about this process of transformation and metamorphoses, the ability to find the magical quality within the mundane reality.

David Blackburn was born in Huddersfield in Yorkshire on 22 June 1939. His father Wilfrid Blackburn (1906–66) ran a small family interior decorating business and is remembered by his son as a quiet self-contained man, a dreamer, who came from a Baptist background. In many ways he appeared to be a rather solitary person, whose life was bounded by religion, work and homelife, who found a release in music, playing the piano reasonably well, and in painting watercolours, gardening and cycling.

His mother Nora (1907–93) was a Methodist, who was happy with her lot and certain of her path in life. David was a lone child, and while there was talk of adoption, this amounted to nothing.

The war, for David, almost entirely bypassed Huddersfield and his earliest memories were of a lonely childhood, where he felt more of an observer of life than a participant. He recalls the "Awful blackness of urban life and the moors were the great escape from darkness into light."[7] At home he felt that he could never talk about feelings — there was a security, but without particular focus, and happiness was found more in self-absorption in a fantasy world than participation in family life. He went to the local Crosland Moor Primary School and then continued at the

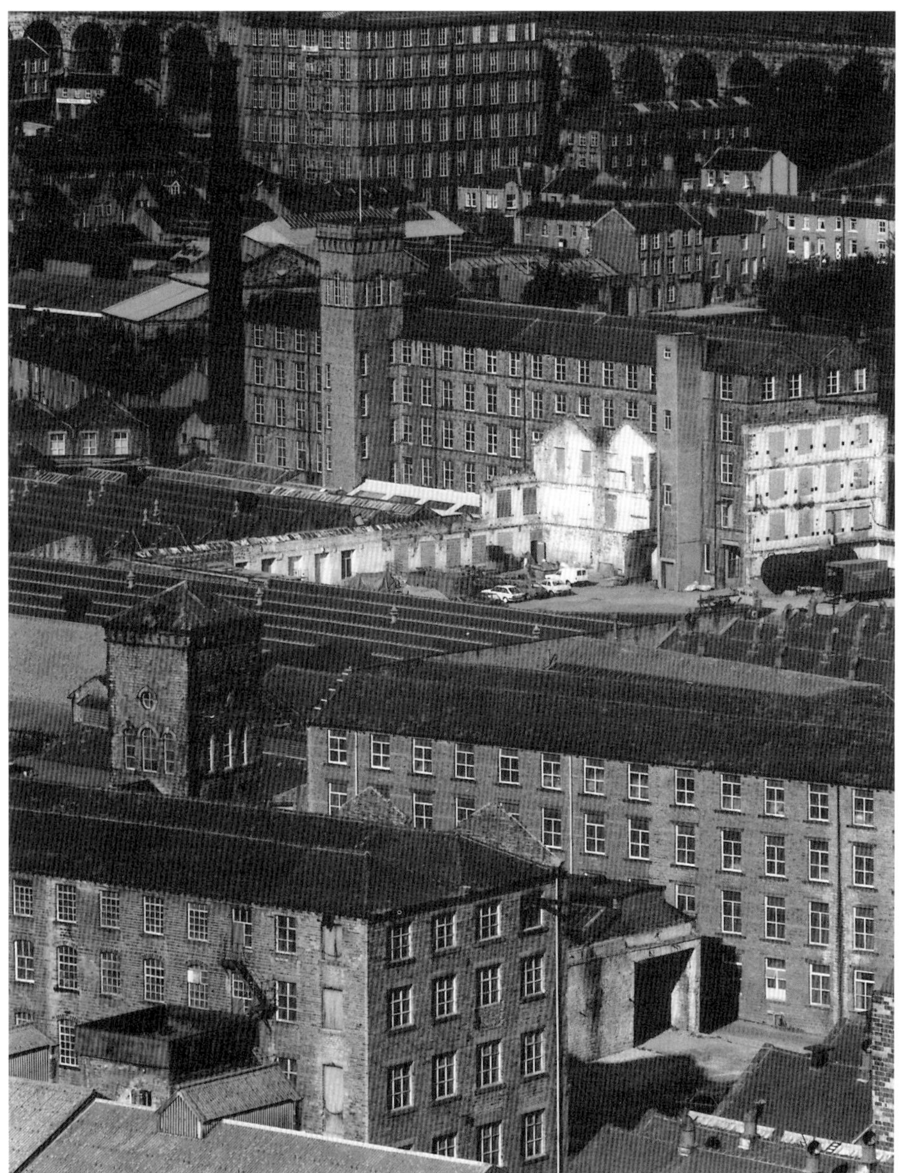

Richard Littlewood
Milnsbridge — Huddersfield, 1987

Junior School in the same building. At eleven he won a scholarship to Huddersfield College, the leading grammar school in the town, and five years later enrolled at the Huddersfield School of Art.[8] Academically, mathematics was one of his great strengths and loves, and this was in part superseded by a passion for athletics in which he trained as a runner and competed as a junior for the English Schools.

The decision to go to an art school was in part a response to winning a nine guinea headmaster's prize for drawing at the age of fifteen, and in part the promise of learning the necessary skills to make a living as a textile designer. He had an instinctive gift for colour and texture and a superb sense of line which his teachers recognised and guided him into the textile course. In John Hindle, an RCA trained artist who was in charge of textiles, David Blackburn found an inspiring teacher. He felt that more than anything else he had acquired a respect for materials, a sense of history and the technical skills necessary with which one could describe the world. The artists whom he grew to admire most at the time were the ones who helped him to sort out his attitude to the landscape. They included Dürer, Sutherland, Munch, Nolde, Friedrich, Blake, Palmer and David Jones. There was a desire for art to have a sense of what could be termed archeological accuracy and at the same time a quality of passion and intensity.

At the age of twenty his move to the RCA signified a break on many important levels. Physically it was a move away from the enclosed space of home, Huddersfield and the landscape which he loved and around which he had started to create a private mythology. It was also a break with an essentially monkish existence, where he had developed what could be termed an animistic relationship to nature and light, and he was plunged into the vastness of an urban environment, first living in Earls Court and then at Kew Gardens. As far as his art was concerned, in Huddersfield he had spent most of his time acquiring the skills to describe the world which surrounded him. In London there was a subtle shift of emphasis; he wished to describe his own feelings — the intense emotional life, which he wanted to communicate through the metaphor of the landscape. The landscape of the north became the inner fields of his mind through which he set out to convey his feelings about living in central London. "What I was looking for were marks which could in some ways be equated with the human figure, but remained as marks drawn from the landscape."[9] This was accompanied by a realisation that textile design was not to be a central interest in his life and that drawing, which had always occupied the major proportion of his time, was to be his principal medium of expression. There was also the understanding that his path in art was set and that the RCA was a facility to use, rather than an institution from which one could learn. He recalls that for him the RCA was a big disappointment, and although he developed a friendship with David Hockney and a number of other students, he perceived that there was a general sense of apathy to art and beauty and few shared his sense of excitement.

He returned to Huddersfield roughly every three weeks mainly because he missed the landscape. London for him was a wonderful experimental laboratory, a place with the great collections of art, especially the Victoria and Albert Museum, the British Museum and the Courtauld Collection. He spent much of his time seeking out objects which he felt had a sense of magic about them, like the V & A's collection of Persian miniatures, and then he would return to the Yorkshire landscape and the search for the magical images, the language and the forms through which he could order his feelings about what excited him in London.

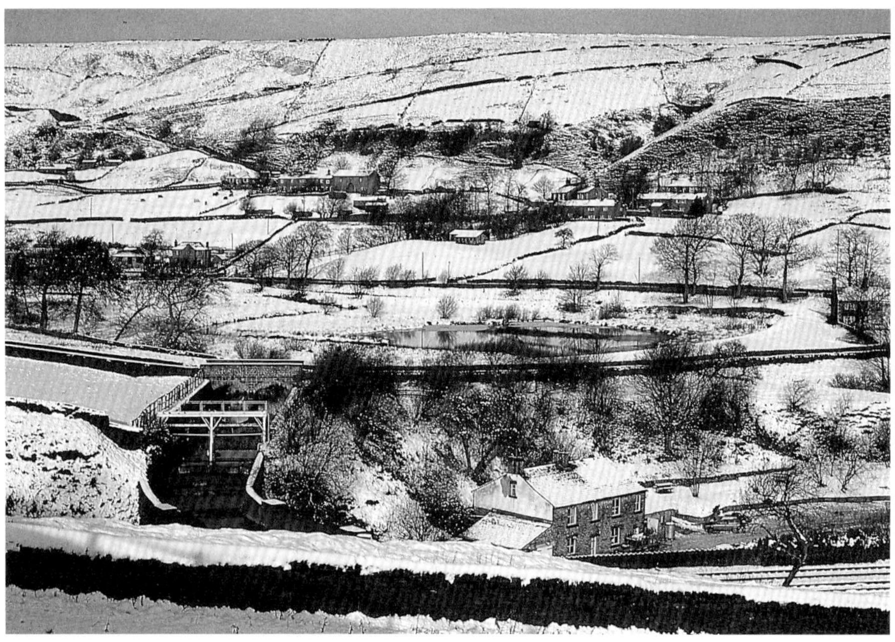

Marsden — West Yorkshire, *photograph: W. Fediw*

A seminal influence at the time was Blackburn's encounter in 1961 with Patrick White's novel *Riders in the chariot*. White appeared as an example of an artist who could create a "personal mythology" in which the big universal themes could be treated on an intimate scale. In Patrick White he found a way in which a personal narrative could develop, where the figures in the landscape served both to tell a story and serve as metaphors for something else and in that way relating the author's philosophy and feelings. The whole was permeated with a sense of magic and grandeur, yet it never seemed to lose sight of the specific landscape within which it was set. Also in White there was an example of a writer who could create his own path, rather than following a fashionable trend. Three years later, when he met White in Australia, he discovered that the admiration was mutual and the writer acquired a number of his pictures.

The person who proved instrumental in Blackburn's artistic development was Gerhart Frankl, an Austrian Jewish *emigré* painter who had settled in London. In Frankl he found a father figure, a person who appeared as a "complete artist", one who lived his art, came from a tradition of Jewish internationalism and, despite a certain isolation, had an intensity and expansiveness. He met Frankl in 1960 through Basil Taylor, the librarian at the RCA, and a very close relationship formed almost immediately. Frankl in his work at the time had developed a method of combining pastel and gouache to produce his colour drenched images of mountains, heavily imbued with the sense of other-worldliness. Blackburn had for several years been working in black chalk, occasionally experimenting with oil pastels and watercolours. The impact of Frankl's work was in part the introduction to colour pastels and their ability to form fluid, ambiguous veils of colour. It was during his time at the RCA when he was seeing Frankl on a weekly basis that he gradually abandoned all other media and started to work exclusively in pastel. A possible source for his use of oil pastels may have been the work of Keith Vaughan, whom Blackburn admired as a colourist.

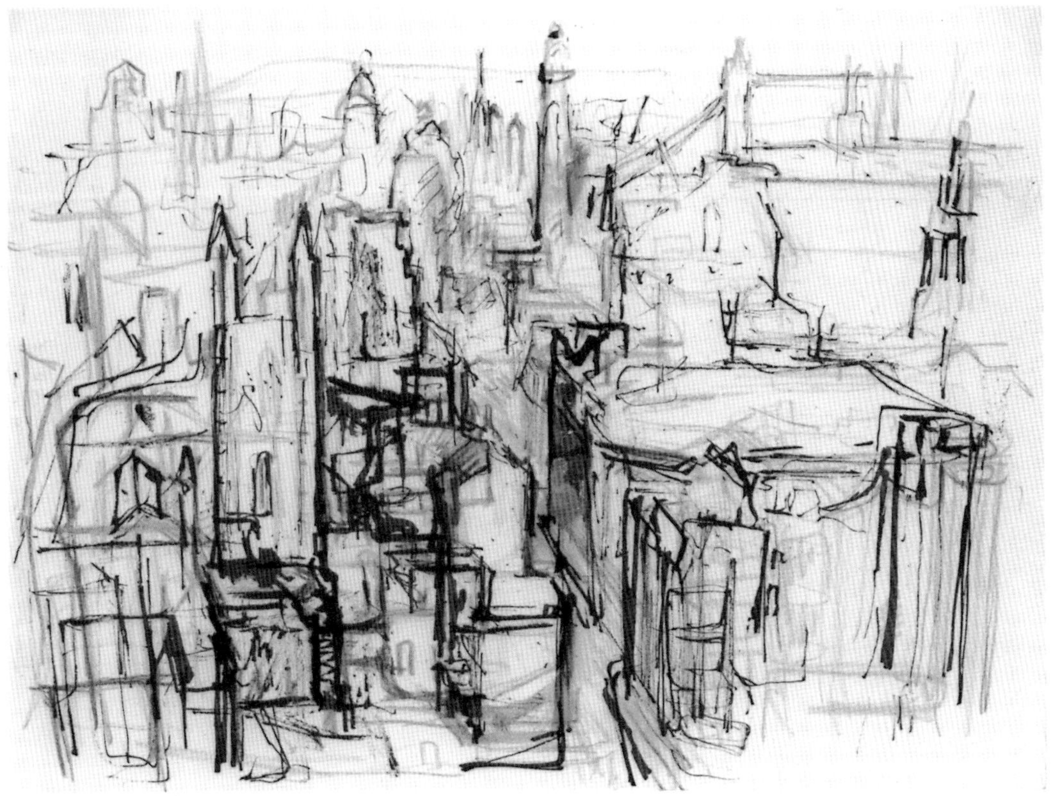

Gerhart Frankl (1905–65)
Sketch Book — London, 1949–53
Ink & Pastel
27cm × 37cm
Collection: Gerhart Frankl Memorial Trust

The other significant person who appeared in his life while he was studying in London was Lord Clark. In 1962 he met Sir Kenneth Clark, as he was then, who showed enormous enthusiasm for his work and became a major patron and one of his most articulate champions. Blackburn had made a number of unfashionable decisions. Both by choosing the landscape and pastels on paper as his exclusive medium, he had chosen to swim against the tide. The visionary landscape was generally deemed as anachronistic, while works on paper and the intimate scale which this implied, automatically in prevailing curatorial practice made the work appear unworthy of being regarded as a major artistic statement. His contemporary students at the RCA were generally painting on a monumental scale, making loud statements to echo those coming from the New York School. Kenneth Clark recognised in Blackburn's work a quiet strength and power and later wrote in anticipation of one of his exhibitions that he would "tell everyone interested in art that . . . you are one of the few living painters worth looking at. So I hope that it will have some effect, but it is very difficult to swim against the tide."[10] Clark, who had written one of the most perceptive histories of landscape art,[11] appeared to Blackburn to speak from the grand tradition of art history; which gave him confidence to continue on the solitary path which he had selected.

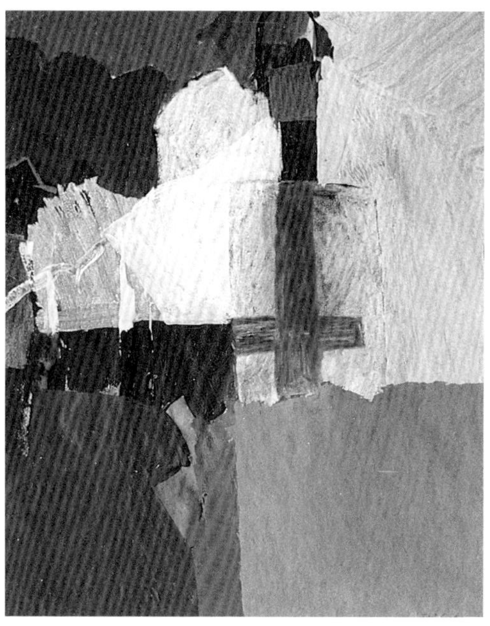

Keith Vaughan
Landscape with a Church, 1972
Gouache
$11^1/_2" \times 9^1/_2"$
Private Collection

David Blackburn's drawings at the time were largely in black chalk and were experiments with visionary landscapes. They were as much about mood as about the accidental forms discovered in the landscape and their anthropomorphic associations. Strange, twisted and gnarled tree forms open up a whole range of associations with human figures and there is the process of metamorphoses recorded where a new form is born through feeling. It is a process of metaphysical transformation, the search for something which is always present, even if unseen. In these early works the transformation was almost always direct, at times overstated, the human element was on the surface ready to stress that the subject was as much the human

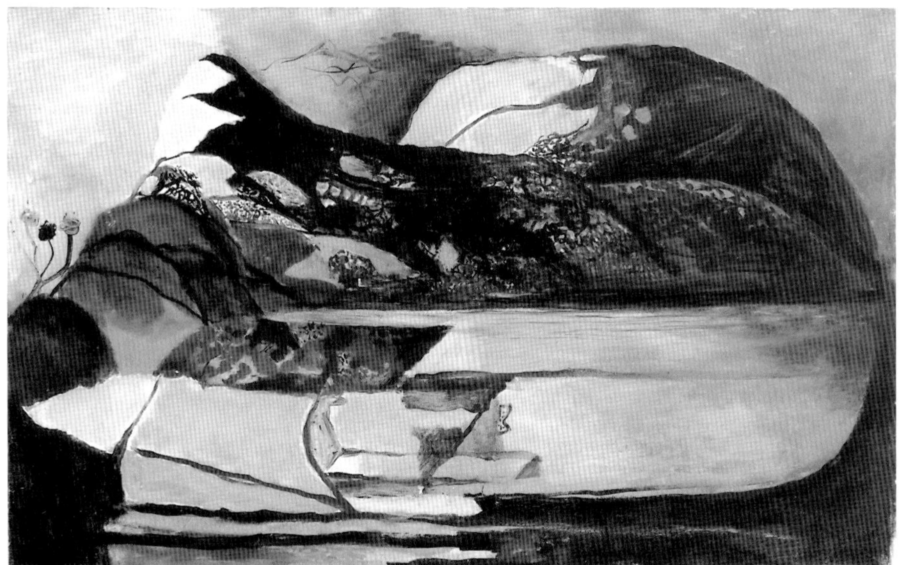

Graham Sutherland, OM
Black Landscape, 1939–40
Oil and sand on canvas
32½" × 52"

condition as a study of the landscape. The black and white stressed the uncompromising intensity of the work and pointed to the common heritage of Dürer, Blake, Palmer, the biomorphic forms of Sutherland and the textural marks of Tàpies.

David Blackburn graduated from the RCA in June 1962 and immediately applied for teaching posts in art schools in English speaking countries, while he himself set off for an extended tour of the art museums of Europe. It was an obsessive search for art objects which he felt had a quality of magic about them. At this stage in his life it was the German Gothic and Renaissance masters, as well as the nineteenth century Romantics, who seemed to have the greatest relevance to his work, rather than the painters of the School of Paris, although he did admire the great colourists Matisse and Bonnard. He also found himself increasingly drawn to the work of the Italian painters Giorgio Morandi and Giorgio de Chirico. It is characteristic of David Blackburn's working method to look intensely at the marks of other artists seeking in them a sense of history which would somehow legitimise his own process of mark making.

On his return to Britain late in 1962, he found two offers of employment, one in the US and the other in Australia. He accepted the latter and arrived in Melbourne early the following year. This was the first of a string of visits to Australia, a country with which he established a special relationship. A valid parallel

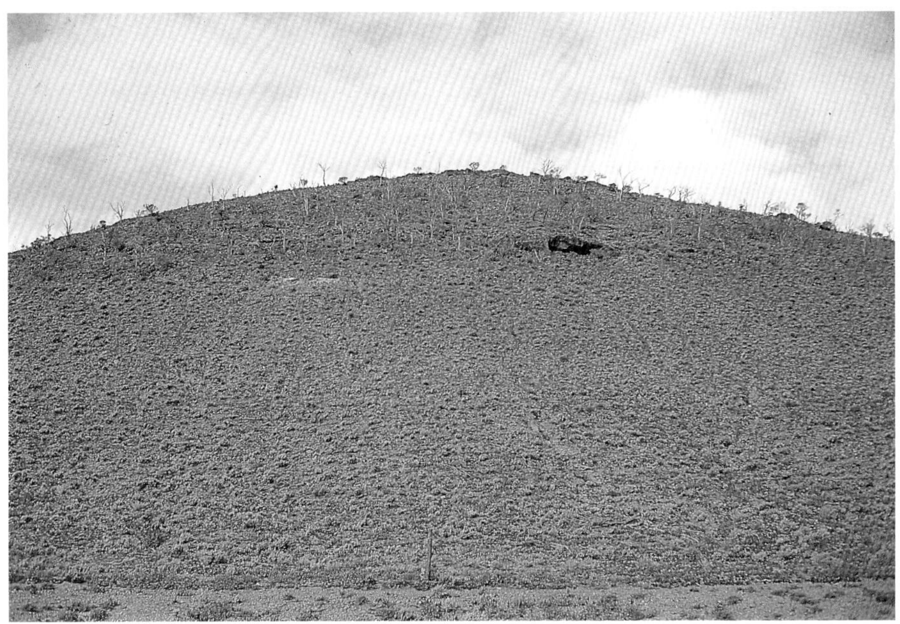

Australian Hillside

may be drawn with Sutherland's discovery of the Riviera. Sutherland visited the Riviera for the first time in 1947 and was struck by the exotic, harsh, arid, yet spectacular landscape with its colour saturation and intensity of light which were so unfamiliar to him. He returned to this landscape annually in search of motifs and new imagery which continued to feed his art, only to be later supplemented with trips to the Veneto in Italy.[12] When Blackburn arrived in Australia, like Sutherland, he encountered a landscape totally unfamiliar to him, a vast featureless landscape bathed in a strange light of bleached intensity. He later reflected "If you are a romantic painter concerned with transforming the real world into your own language, then the Australian landscape poses a particular challenge. It is a landscape which has virtually never been painted by Europeans, there are no precedents which makes it easier for the landscape painter to work from. If you are in a historical tradition and you are painting in England, the landscape has its vocabulary and morphology and this conditions your own language, as it has been painted so many times and you are aware of the precedents, every hill, rock and clump of trees begs for comparison in another artist's work. In Australia I am discovering the landscape afresh, because of its enormous scale and flatness. No white man has ever painted all of it and it is easier for me to overlay a myth on it, to invest my marks with a sense of magic, yet to relate directly to the landscape."[13]

The twenty-four year old David Blackburn found in Melbourne on his arrival a stimulating and challenging art scene. He was fortunate that he had been appointed to teach part-time at the Royal Melbourne Institute of Technology

(RMIT), an art school which was rapidly becoming recognised as one of the leading art institutions in the country. It was also the start of the sixties art boom in Australia with sell-out exhibitions and a lively debate in the Press the order of the day. With Sidney Nolan, Arthur Boyd and Brett Whiteley, Australian art was also now achieving an international reputation. Perhaps the factor which was more significant than any other for David Blackburn was that landscape painting for various historical reasons was the principal artistic tradition in Australian art. So, for a young landscape painter just emerging from graduate studies, Australia appeared as a Mecca for his work, a place where landscape art was taken seriously. His letters back to England at the time are permeated with a euphoric enthusiasm for Australia, an admiration for the exotic scenery and the new qualities of colour and light.

Although he expressed this fascination with the Australian landscape, the drawings themselves reflected relatively little change. He continued to work primarily in black chalk with the drawings appearing as detailed biomorphic studies of elements taken from nature. Australian art critics commenting on his first solo exhibition in July 1965, were quick to note this. One wrote "in his black chalk drawings of leaves, bark and twisted roots, [he] studies nature intensively in order to uncover her hidden language of time and mortality. The fascination of these black drawings lies in the double-edged intention: to cling to the natural image while wrestling its moral secret from it."[14] Essentially this echoed Kenneth Clark's interpretation that "landscape painting, like all forms of art, was an act of faith . . .

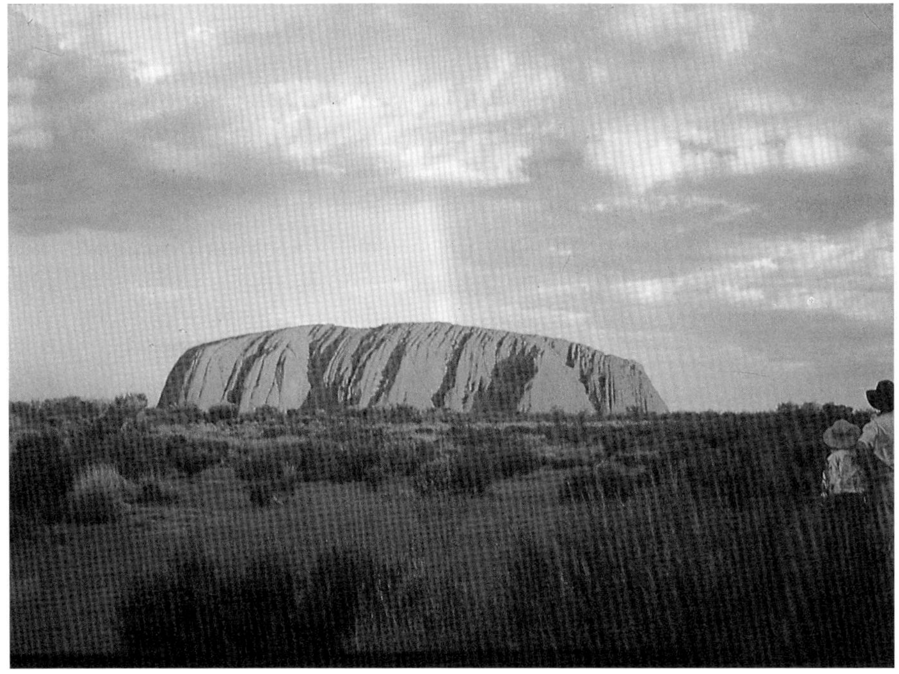

Ayers Rock

the belief that the inherent sanctity of nature had a purifying and uplifting effect on those who opened their hearts to her influence."[15]

Blackburn's first trip to Australia lasted over three years and he divided his time between teaching life drawing for one and a half days a week at RMIT and general drawing and printmaking for one day a week at Prahran Technical College.[16] All of this came to an abrupt halt in mid-1966 when news reached him that his father had suffered a stroke and was gravely ill. He immediately departed for home. Looking back at his work during the first Australian period, there is a certain culmination of ideas which he had started to explore earlier in Britain. While the focus was on small specific details derived from immediate observation, the transformation was into symbolic images which in a microcosmic sense stood for universal themes. Titles frequently bore traces of a literary process of thought and touched on ideas of apocalypse, genesis, life and death and creation. It was in Australia that he commenced and largely completed the first major series of his *oeuvre* — the first *Creation* series.

Blackburn has always worked in series with the last drawing containing within itself clues to the beginning of the next. The twenty-one black chalk drawings of the first *Creation* series, executed between 1963 and 1966, can be compared with an epic poem, a closed cycle, and in the Homeric sense, each drawing standing for a separate verse or incident, having an autonomy and independence, while at the same time intricately interwoven within the texture of the whole. The cycle begins with the separation of light from darkness and ends with the extinguishing of light and the darkness of the Apocalypse. On one level the series is literal in its narrative content, intense, dramatic and tragic in its resolution. It also lends itself to be read on an autobiographical level with the descending darkness foreboding the death of the artist's father. It is a youthful work, a creation of high Romanticism, where the artist is obsessed with his own inspirational responses to the world, and, with almost a messianic zeal seems determined to change the world. For his imagery he draws freely on a broad tradition of art history, there are echoes of Bosch, Breughel and Dürer and he prominently employs William Blake's haunting image of *Ancient of Days* and Leonardo da Vinci's drawing of man as the measure of all things.[17] The whole is conceived in terms of a polarity, of light and darkness, life and death, a beginning and an end. The mechanical forms of clocks and dividers constantly point to this separation in time and space and to the struggle of human endeavour pitted against the prevailing forces of nature.

The first *Creation* series was in some respects David Blackburn's most ambitious work ever and while in some of its drawings, it suffers through overstatement,

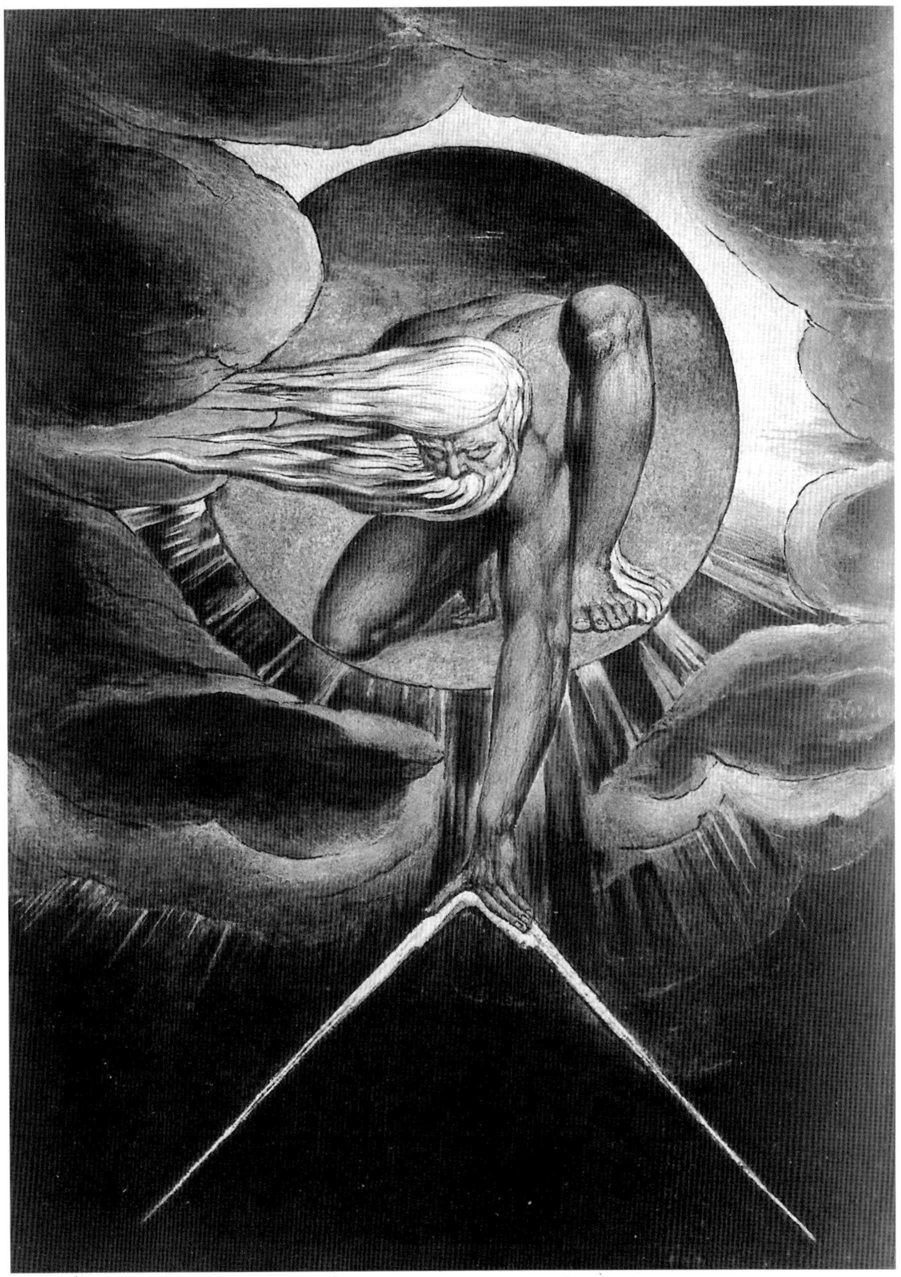

William Blake
The Ancient of Days,
Pen and Ink
Collection: The Whitworth Art Gallery, University of Manchester

ultimately it is rescued through its vigour and freshness. It reads very much as a single breath of creation, the triumph of the heroic individual and the melancholy visionary imagination. The challenge in much of his subsequent work was to somehow retain the freshness and that myriad of unexpected discoveries and associations, yet to distil and order the marks, to retain the passion, but somehow to relate it in tranquillity.

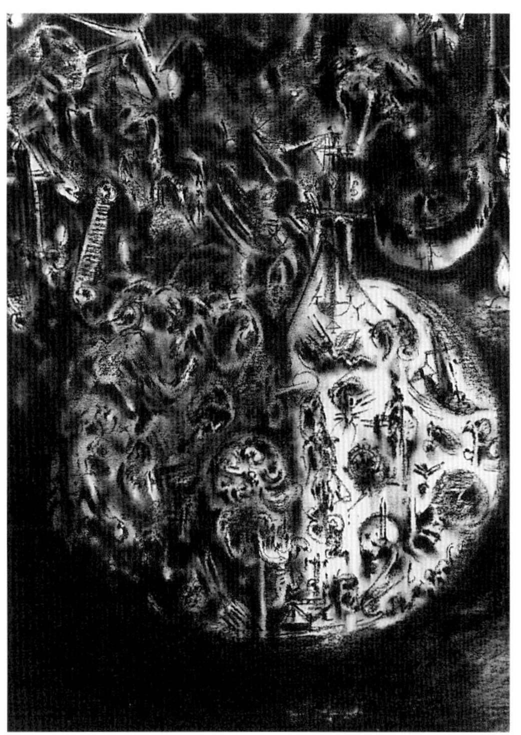

David Blackburn
The Creation Series, 1963–66
Detail: No. 7 — Light divided from darkness — life
Pastel
15" × 10 3/4"
Private Collection

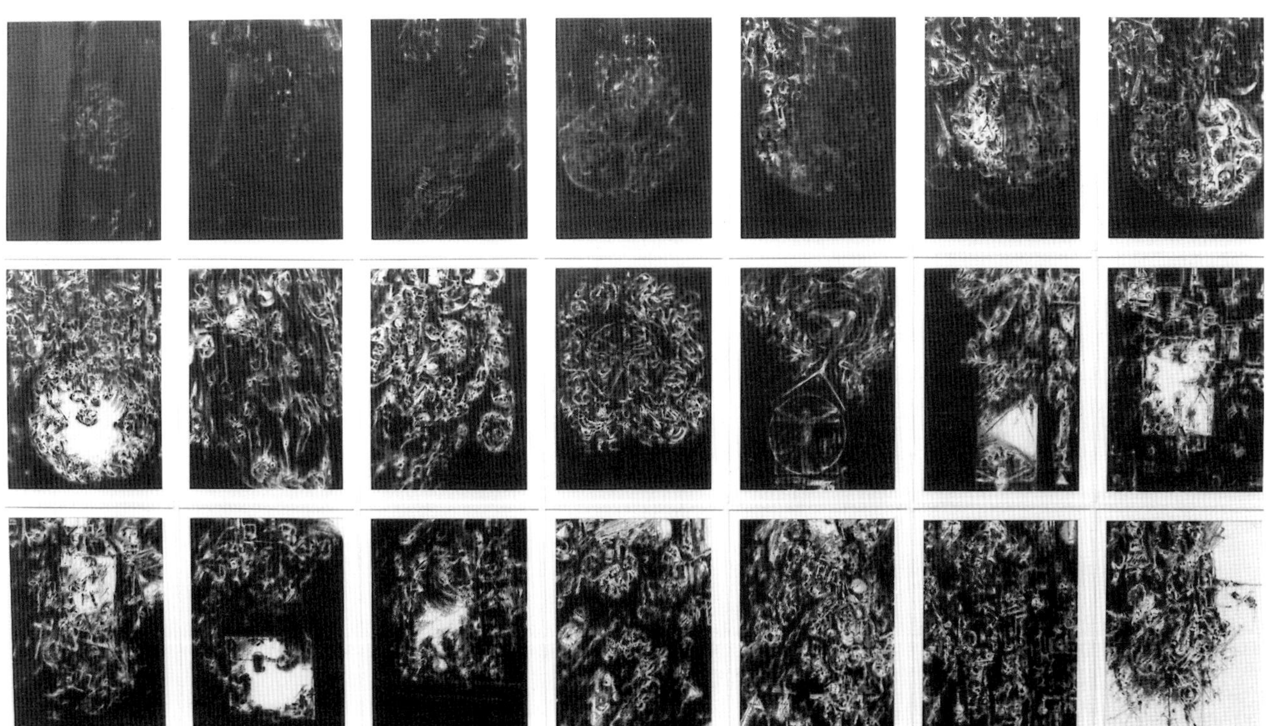

David Blackburn
The Creation Series, 1963–66
Pastel
$60'' \times 96^1/_2''$
individually $15'' \times 10^3/_4''$
Private Collection

On his return to England in mid-1966 he commenced teaching drawing part-time at various art schools including Batley, Huddersfield and at Manchester University. He also almost immediately embarked on a major new series of drawings, *The Metamorphoses*. If most of his drawings up to 1966 were derived from organic forms, *The Metamorphoses* series is about transformations within interior spaces. They hint at enclosures, with references to cages, screens, doors and entrances. There is the unmistakable influence of Francis Bacon and his early studies of figures in a landscape and within enclosures, the strange screen devices and his brilliant early manifestation of agony and faith in his triptych *Three studies for figures at the base of a Crucifixion*.[18] As in the first *Creation* series there is still the preoccupation with making a comment on the human condition, and there is a heightened eschatological meaning with the whole series charged with an autobiographical significance: the death of his father late in 1966 from a second stroke. If with the earlier series the parallel was with epic poetry, here the concepts are more symbolic and abstract. There is a very conscious attempt made to create a religious painting, one which would deal with birth and resurrection, but in such a way that the human figure itself would not be present. The screens, boxes, cages, doors, altars and the vague skeletal figures emerging from the refining fire, all are in a state of change and weave their own mysterious mythology. If there is a literary source for this series, it is no longer Biblical, but points to Patrick White and the notions of change and transformation which are prevalent in many of his writings.

The Metamorphoses series, perhaps more than any other in David Blackburn's work, can in retrospect be viewed as something of a watershed. His earlier organic studies have been abandoned in favour of much richer and more complex pictorial structures. They are far more subtle and ambiguous drawings, where literary content may be alluded to, but there is no trace of the illustrative. Colour for the first time is allowed to play a decisive role in the final drawings of the series — strong, dramatic, yet lyrical. Also, increasingly he was receiving critical acclaim.

Colour, which appeared only in the final drawings of *The Metamorphoses*, plays an increasingly important role in his subsequent work. The second *Creation* cycle, completed in 1969, was composed of seven triptychs[19] mounted within a single outer frame. In this cycle the Apocalyptic darkness has lifted and it is no longer conceived as the struggle of light emerging from darkness only to once more be engulfed by the void. Now in the *Creation* cycle appears a Trinitarian symbol of three red lines which moves over the waters in the first drawings, while in the final triptych, there is an image of peace — three seascapes which are tranquil and eternal, which relate to the seventh day when God was pleased and rested.

Apart from the introduction of colour, the new work also saw a subtle change in the development of technique. The black pastel drawings were on very flat heavy white German watercolour paper and the surface was allowed to breathe, as in the watercolour technique, with bits of the white of the paper showing through. This created a certain spatial tension between the paper and the black pastel which sat on top of the surface. In the colour drawings, particularly as they emerged in the early seventies, he used a heavier and more textured paper, where a layer of pastel tended to entirely cover the surface of the sheet with the colour bleeding into the paper. The four sides of the sheet were stuck down with strips of tape which were removed when the drawing was finished to create crisp, straight hard edges. On this fluid layer of colour pastel, further layers were applied, some smudged and rubbed into the surface with fingers, other blocks of pastel colour were sometimes worked up against a sheet of paper which facilitated sharply delineated colour planes, and occasional surface marks were left as if to float on the surface. Blackburn's process of work conceptually has much in common with that employed by the Abstract Expressionist painters. The surface on which he works can be compared to an arena in which the artist encounters his medium and the trails of energy stemming from this encounter are preserved in the finished state of the work capturing the process of the emergence of form.

This technique of manipulation of pastel went considerably beyond the one developed by Gerhart Frankl in his pastel and gouache landscape studies and moved the whole medium into new and largely uncharted territory. Pastel was no longer sitting on the surface of the paper, but was worked into the paper to produce what could be termed "deep colour". It was an enormously flexible technique which created wonderful, sonorous colour reflexes on top of which could be suspended marks of great subtlety and sensitivity. This technique also required very intense periods of concentration, with Blackburn working in a four to six hour stretch, usually returning to the same drawing several days in a row. This process of work also meant that it could only be carried out in the studio, so that one or two days a week were set aside for sketching with pastel or charcoal from nature, while the rest of the time was spent in the studio working on his dissolving colour visions.

In February 1971 David Blackburn journeyed for a second time to Australia, this time spending several months as a visiting lecturer at the University of Melbourne. It was at this time that he realised that on his previous visit to Australia, although he was struck by the novelty of the landscape, he had failed to come to any sort of understanding of it. At that stage he was really "an Englishman trying to find an English landscape in Australia [and that] in those three years he did not see

Australia at all, and if he had had a garden, he would have put a fence around it and planted English flowers."[20] This was a common phenomenon amongst English artists coming to Australia. Back in the early nineteenth century, artists such as Thomas Watling and Joseph Lysett saw "the wild scenery of Australia in her pristine state" as capable of much improvement, based on the English model.[21] Subsequent English visiting painters continued to interpret the landscape of Australia within the conventions of the English landscape tradition. On this visit to Australia Blackburn for the first time travelled to the red interior and into the central deserts to discover a rich repertoire of imagery which was to inform his work for the next decade.

It was during this second visit to Australia that David Blackburn commenced his *Creation of Landscape* series which was to preoccupy him between 1971 and 1975 and was to become one of his most important achievements in the visionary landscape tradition. Two important innovations contributed to the work. The first was the discovery in Australia of the heavy Arches paper which quite literally soaked in the pastel to produce an unmatched luminosity with rich internal glow. The second was the encounter with the Russo-Byzantine tradition of hagiographical icons. Within this tradition in the centre of the icon there is a large image of the saint, while in a band around the border there is a whole series of narrative scenes which contained episodes from his life. It was an ideal format for an "icon of the landscape", a celebration of the transcendental quality of the landscape, its sense of spirituality and magic, an "other-worldliness" which depicted a heaven on earth. In the large *The Creation of Landscape* panel,[22] four large drawings, which closely link together, form the central image, while around the edges, sixteen separate drawings appear as a form of symbolic narrative which celebrates the emergence of a glowing landscape vision.

John Ruskin, in his discussion of his personal response to the landscape, in one of the most lyrical passages in *Modern Painters,* noted, "Although there was no definite religious sentiment mingled with it, there was a continual perception of Sanctity in the whole of nature, from the slightest thing to the vastness; an instinctive awe, mixed with delight; an indefinable thrill, such as we sometimes imagine to indicate the presence of a disembodied spirit."[23] It is this ineffable feeling for the "continual perception of Sanctity in the whole of nature" which permeates this panel. There is just a hint of the creation myth, with the desert-like vastness of the central panel, with stones casting shadows from the glow of a mysterious light source, to the watery aerial visions and magic flying carpets of the drawings which surround this centre. The panel is rich in luminous greens and blues with scattered tiny specks of intense light like glowing coals, as if scattered little

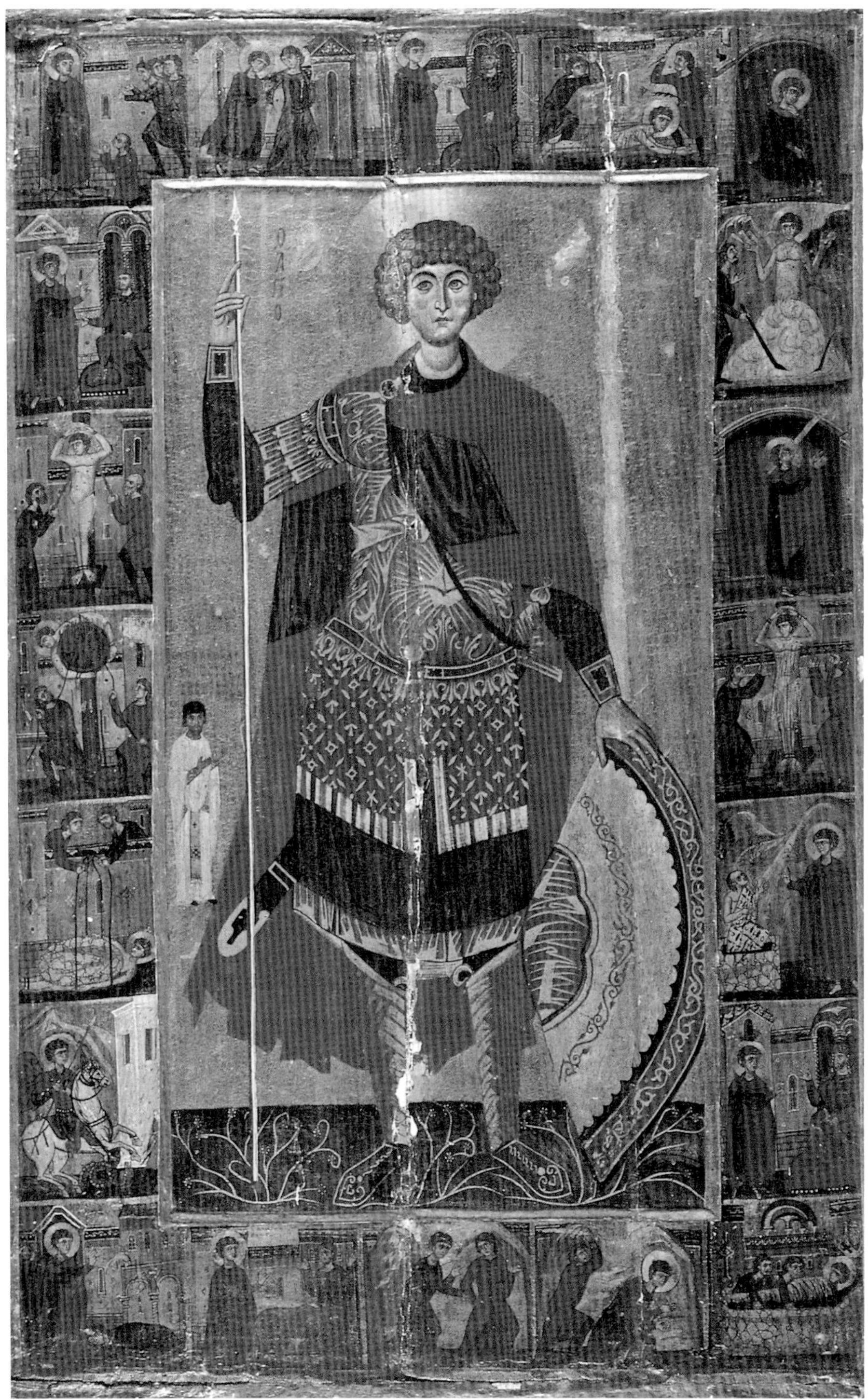

Sinai Icon with Saint George, first half — 13th Century
127cm × 78.5cm
Private Collection

pockets of energy. There is a lyrical beauty, but one which is devoid of even a trace of sentimentality or a literary content. There is also a quality of something which is haunting and mysterious, a very subtle suggestion that in the moment of the ecstasy of creation lie concealed the seeds of the Apocalypse, that even in a paradisal vision, the eschatological nightmare of Bosch lies somewhere below the surface.

By the early seventies Blackburn's standing as an artist was becoming established amongst the British and Australian art critics. In England, following the early encouragement from Sir Herbert Read, he received strong support from Kenneth Clark, Humphrey Brooke and Lord Eccles, the British Minister for the Arts, all of whom publicly praised his art and privately collected it. From 1970 onwards he held exhibitions with Agnews, the prestigious gallery in London, the shows being generally well-received and attracting favourable comment. In Australia, on his first visit in 1963, he won the support of Professor Joseph Burke, the first Professor of Art history in Australia and a man of enormous culture, warmth and erudition. His early exhibitions with the Argus Gallery in Melbourne and the Watters Gallery in Sydney were supplemented in 1973 by exhibitions with the Joseph Brown Gallery in Melbourne, one of Australia's most respected and important galleries. The Australian critic Robert Hughes was enthusiastic about his work, while Patrick McCaughey, one of the more articulate voices in Australian art criticism, was lavish in his praise.[24]

The question nevertheless arises why, in spite of the praise from critics and the support of some of the leading figures active in the visual arts, David Blackburn's work was not launched into international prominence, as was, for example, the work of his Yorkshire contemporary, David Hockney. The explanation lies probably in two main areas. The first is with the medium — pastel on paper. Generally amongst art curators in the twentieth century working in the Western European tradition there has been a prejudice against work on paper as constituting a major artistic statement. Oil paintings, particularly on a monumental scale, and large sculptural pieces, were seen as the only artistic forms worthy of museum attention, while works on paper when they were collected were seen, more often than not, as an adjunct to an artist's serious activities, or as studies towards a major work. The second reason lies in the nature of Blackburn's philosophy of art. By choosing to work within a tradition, he was viewed as moving against the tide of mainstream modernism as constructed on the Francophile model. Modernism, in one of its aspects, has been interpreted as a series of denials and limitations; for example, the rejection of mimesis and of any representational intent, the rejection of three-dimensional space, rejection of traditional materials and so forth. Although an artist in a post-modernist world has the whole tradition of art history at his or her fingertips to plunder, these acts of plunder, even when they involve historic resuscitation, are within an assumed framework of a historical progression. Here the underlying assumption is that the tyranny of tradition has been destroyed together with the myth of originality, and this presupposes that one of the major functions of art has been the negation of tradition, change and innovation.[25] The strength of David Blackburn's art lies precisely in the fact that he has chosen to be an innovator within a great tradition of art history, the tradition of the personal visionary landscape, rather than setting out to simply negate this tradition through a nihilistic stance. This attitude to art, like his preference to work on paper in pastels on an intimate scale, has ensured that his art has been placed outside the popularly promoted construct of the international mainstream.

Although the diaristic concept is a popular one in contemporary art, it is normally associated with the idea of art as autobiography and is particularly popular in some forms of feminist art practice. Blackburn's concept of art as a diary is much closer to that involved in the work of Giorgio Morandi where through his continual series of pots and bottles he establishes a sense of intimacy, which is deeply moving, personal and profound. The Italian critic Cesare Brandi back in 1952 brilliantly characterised this when he wrote "Morandi's painting style unfolds with time, tacitly faithful to itself and yet forever changing, through variations that are almost imperceptible at the apex but increasingly conspicuous towards the base — perhaps it is like an 'olive branch' in the midst of modern painting?"[26] Blackburn's use of the metaphor of the landscape involves a similar self-identification as in Morandi's use of the still life, where a very personal emotional content is used to inform the drawings. While each drawing, like a Morandi painting, has an autonomy in its own right, when seen as a collective series, there is a gradual progression from sheet to sheet and a growing spiritual intensity.

This diaristic process of work meant that it was an internal, even metaphysical, landscape which appeared in his drawings, rather than one related to his immediate environment. In Huddersfield, he could produce drawings which breathed the intensity of light and the red glow of the central Australian deserts. In Australia, some of his drawings celebrated the luxuriant greens of the Colne Valley, with floating magical carpets which reflected his growing fascination with flying. Each drawing would continue where the previous one left off, creating an extensive series which would sometimes span a number of years. In fact, his whole *oeuvre* could be viewed as a single series of work, one continuous diary of creation.

The most immediate experience of Australia was felt in the new colour range, especially of the red interior, and in the new iconography of monolithic anthills, desert horizons strewn with stones casting long shadows and the sparse featureless clumps of vegetation. Perhaps more significantly, there was a major formal influence on his art, the impact of the landscape vision of the Australian artist Fred Williams. Blackburn recalls that on his first encounter with the paintings and etchings of Fred Williams in 1963, his response was one of bewildered hostility. "When I first saw Fred Williams's work, I did not like it. I did not think that it was 'true', whatever true may mean, but with seeing more of the landscape I realised how true they were. It became a two-way respect, you respected the paintings formally and you admired them as they had a truth to the landscape."[27] When he first came to Australia, he was an Englishman in Australia trying to weave an English sense of myth on what he perceived as a new and largely uncharted terrain. The artists who at that stage helped him the most to come to grips with the Australian landscape were other English, Anglo-Australian and European painters, particularly John Glover, Arthur Streeton, Tom Roberts, Conrad Martens and Louis Buvelot, who essentially interpreted the Australian landscape within the conventions of Barbizon naturalism and the Orientalist 'glare aesthetics' devised for conveying the harsh bleaching light of the Middle East. Williams's rendition was radically different.

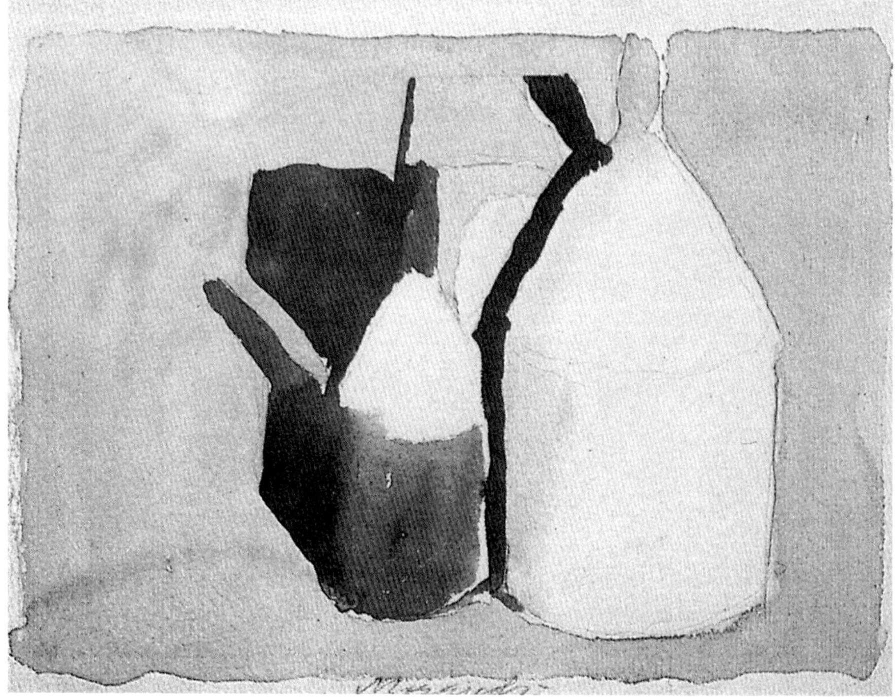

Giorgio Morandi
Natura Morta, 1956
Watercolour
16cm × 24cm
Collection: Morat Institute fur Kunst und Kunstwissenschaft

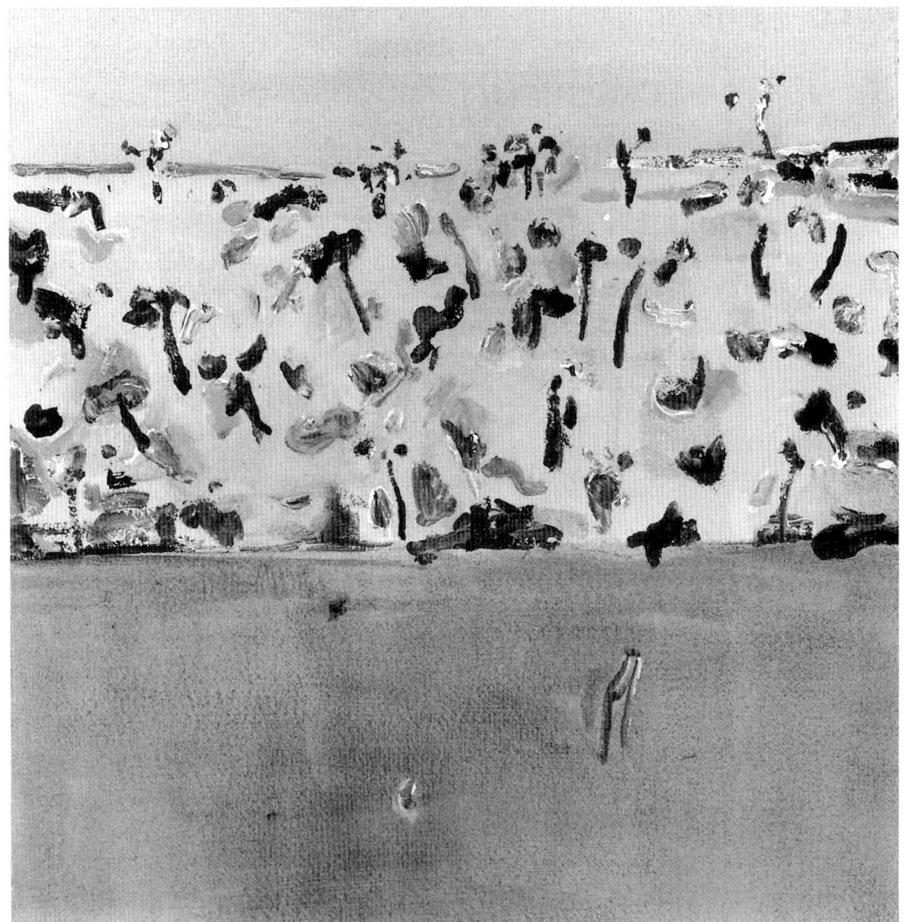

Fred Williams
Study for Lysterfield I, 1971
Synthetic polymer paint on paper
76cm × 55.4cm
Collection: Australian National Gallery, Canberra

Fred Williams (1927–82), who trained as a painter and printmaker in Melbourne and London, returned to Australia from England late in 1956 and commenced to explore what could be termed the unique peculiarities of the Australian landscape. These included its openness, the lack of picturesque focal points, a certain monotony in the undifferentiated high horizons, but at the same time its sense of delicacy, intricacy and complexity. Structurally, he radically flattened out the picture space and reduced the vegetation to highly expressive dabs of colour which appeared as if suspended on the surface rather than anchored in the landscape. In a way he incorporated the cubist planular deconstruction of space and the experience of the Abstract Expressionists' personalised vocabulary of gestural blobs. In some of his work of the later sixties, the experience of minimalism resulted in a certain sparseness in his compositions. Some of his major series of paintings with their related gouaches and etchings, including those of the landscapes at Sherbrooke, You Yangs, Upwey and Lysterfield, created a new morphology of painterly signs and a new way of visualising the Australian landscape which changed the consciousness of a generation of Australian artists.[28]

Throughout the seventies Williams's vision and peculiar method of mark making remained a singularly important source for Blackburn's work. His repeated trips to Australia[29] confirmed for him the validity of Williams's approach. It was a curious decade in his art in that he increasingly identified himself as an Australian artist[30] — in part reflecting the affection which he felt for the country and the recognition which he was receiving there, but also in part a response to the sense of alienation which he experienced in the British art world. Nevertheless, Australian critics and artists inevitably viewed him as an outsider. Patrick McCaughey, in the first important critical assessment of his work, in a perceptive essay remarked that "David Blackburn is an English artist who has the good fortune to belong to a tradition . . . His Australian experience has added something new to it."[31] He centrally located Blackburn's pastel drawings in the English landscape tradition, with the Australian work serving as an extension to this vision. The major Australian painter Russell Drysdale, famed for his images of the Australian interior, after praising Blackburn's Central Australian drawings, which he saw in Agnews in 1972, went on to say "it is good to see *your* view of the place".[32]

A culmination of his work in the seventies came with a retrospective exhibition of his drawings at the University of York which was opened by Lord Clark in October 1978. In his opening remarks Clark advanced an interpretation of Blackburn's work, which set the agenda for almost all subsequent comment. Clark said "It is an exhibition of an artist who is himself absolutely independent from all the tricks, mannerisms and fashions of the art of our time. He is an extraordinarily independent artist. He started as a landscape painter, and landscape is still observable in his drawings, which are really what some of us would call abstract; yet they are not abstract at all because he is a man with an extraordinary sense of life, of situation and character, and he puts all of this into his work in an allusive way. It is difficult sometimes to see what is going on. I was rather baffled looking at his work. Look at his work a long time and I think it will gradually reveal itself to you. Once it had begun to reveal itself to me I came to admire it more and more . . . I don't know any artist to whom I can compare him. He is not a landscape painter, not an abstractionist in the ordinary sense of the word. He is a master of metamorphoses . . . To my mind he is a very distinguished artist . . . a great artist who has not yet received sufficient recognition."[33] Clark here advanced the interpretation of Blackburn as the loner who works outside the established conventions of art practice in Britain of the time, a person who works exclusively from an internal vision and who is independent from all traditions. The fact that he was perceived as such by one of the best informed art historians of the day is in itself of great significance. The tradition of the visionary landscape was seen as either so neglected or obsolete, that no connection between it and David Blackburn's work was drawn.

His drawings of the seventies had an exceptional colouristic richness and vibrancy. The process of work guaranteed that the drawings were worked out on paper, rather than being predetermined in the head. The mark making process of Fred Williams had become totally absorbed into his own idiosyncratic visual morphology with a growing variety in touch, flow and diction. When looking at sequences of his work from this period, there often seems to be a polarity between a literalness of representation and a sense of almost total abstraction. At one end, for example, there are his Yorkshire industrial landscape drawings which generally adopt a high aerial perspective and where it is possible to pick out such specific descriptive details as cooling towers and there is a crispness of articulating line reminiscent of Prunella Clough. At the other end, there are passages of landscape painting where all traces of referential specificity is lost. He himself was conscious of this polarity in his work. "The danger is the two extremes, the drawings are at their worst when they are totally tied to a representation of the real world and they are at their worst when the mark making process has gone so far that the marks have lost their power to relate back to the real world and they have become purely decorative. It is always moving from one extreme to the other."[34]

Perhaps more significantly, not only was he aware of this polarity in his work, but set out in some of his finest drawings of the seventies, particularly his seascapes, to retain a certain specificity while at the same time attempting to purge the landscape image of its directness and immediacy to create a more detached pictorial treatment. As with Tàpies, there was a desire to achieve a certain sensuous presence and a definite spiritual aura, what has been described as "a relationship of tension between the materials employed and the artist's reaction to them, his shaping urge".[35] For Blackburn, Tàpies was the master of the ambiguous poignant mark. His goal was to somehow create this magic of the mark, but to retain a sense of truth to the landscape experience. More than in his earlier drawings, microcosmic conceptions appear in his work with a liberation of the sense of relative scale. A detail of a pattern made by a blade of grass blown over the sand could be enlarged to dominate an entire composition, while a whole expanse of landscape observed while flying could be compressed into a few modest marks. In some of the other drawings, as with Graham Sutherland, it could be a single set of relationships found within a particular landscape, like the relationship between an anthill, its shadow and the horizon, which determines for him the *genius loci* and which is then metamorphosed into pictorial terms.

With the growing frailty in his mother's health, long absences from Huddersfield became increasingly difficult. North America, in contrast to Australia, was only half a dozen hours away in a plane which made short visits several times a year viable; it also meant that he could return to England quickly, at a moment's notice. He made his first journey to the USA in 1980 and returned the following year as a Visiting Professor to Georgetown University in Washington, D.C. For the next decade he visited America and Canada frequently, occasionally a few times a year. The American drawings of the eighties refer to an urban topography, often built around a geometric grid, creating a sense of diagram allowing the viewer to see both the "inside" and "outside" of the landscape. There is a quality of an architectural plan to these landscapes, but no longer are these pictures primarily preoccupied with describing an observed world, but rather alluding to all sorts of

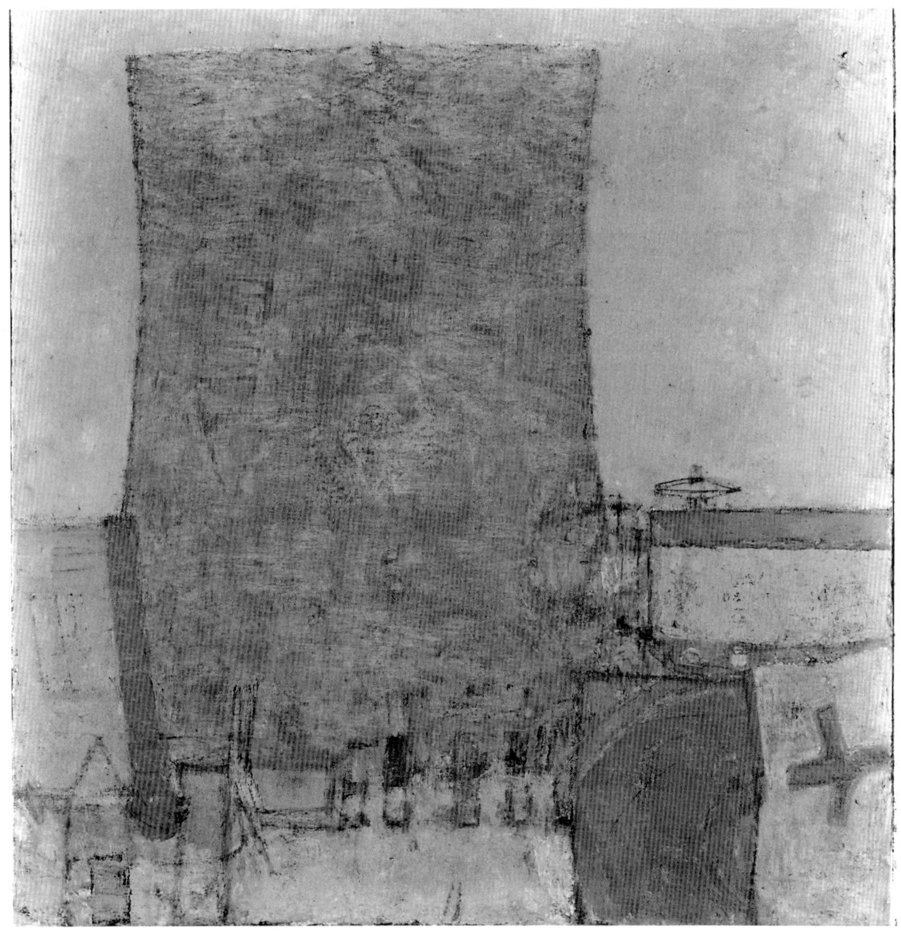

Prunella Clough
Cooling Tower II, 1958
Oil on canvas
38" × 36"

associations. They could be described as beautiful mood pictures with a feeling for geometry. A rather special sort of line appears in these drawings; it is a self-consciously drawn line which exhibits a sense of beautiful calligraphy, it is a line which may not be describing anything specific, but may allude to some feeling like a coastline. While in keeping with the general philosophy of Romantic evocations, the sense of place, the specificity, has almost totally vanished, very much in contrast to the Yorkshire industrial drawings of the late seventies.

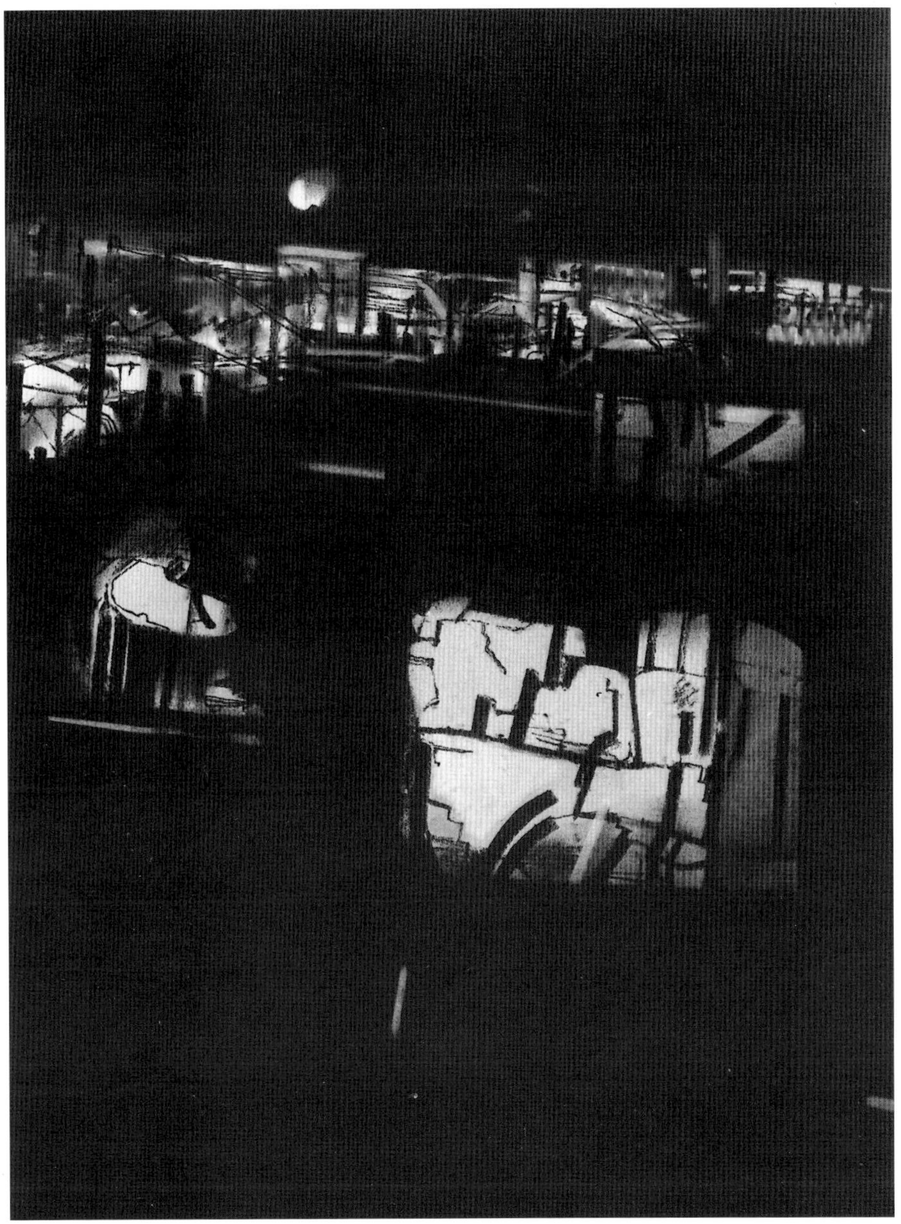

David Blackburn
Rockface with Distant Cityscape, 1975
Black Pastel
25" × 17½"
Private Collection

The American painter and printmaker Richard Diebenkorn, was a major discovery for Blackburn, specifically his *Ocean Park* paintings. Shortly after Diebenkorn shifted to Los Angeles, he commenced in 1967 a large series of paintings to which he gave a generic title *Ocean Park*, which related to a section of the Santa Monica coast in California where he had his studio. There is a certain parallel between Blackburn's and Diebenkorn's treatment of the landscape: both use reductive, non-objective abstractions with an interest in structuralist and formalist concerns as well as a general adherence to Abstract Expressionist theories of picture making. Both use emotionally charged symbols and rich metaphors which operate both in the totality of experience as well as focusing on individual details. Where the two differed was that Diebenkorn disciplined his luminous breathing abstractions through a carefully superimposed linear structure. It was a manner in which spontaneity and closed form could be brought together. Earlier he had commented "At one time the common device of using the super-emotional to get 'in gear' with a painting used to serve me for access to painting too, but I mistrust that now. I think what is more important is a feeling of strength in reserve — tension beneath calm."[37] It was in the *Ocean Park* series that he achieved this "tension beneath calm". These were also a series of landscape paintings which has been described as "description without a place",[37] where the external environment may have been the catalyst, but it is absorbed by its internal self.

The two most important lessons which David Blackburn took from Diebenkorn were the relationship between line and the tonal field and the sense of the descriptive landscape which is largely independent from a specific place. Unlike the experience of Australia almost twenty years earlier, where the landscape vision of Fred Williams swamped his own sensibilities and his own practice came very close to Williams's process of mark making, now Diebenkorn was absorbed into the broader method of work. The series of glowing pastel drawings of architectural windows and prisms of the mid-eighties bring together the experience of England, Australia and America, where line remains playful and beautifully ambiguous and there is a luminosity emanating deep from within. There is the red, mauve and purple colour saturation reminiscent of the Central Australian Desert, lovely floating vibrant patches of green and the ambiguous geometry of line which serves like a membrane, containing and disciplining the form, while opening up planes of illusion.

From the mid-eighties to the early nineties arise a series of monumental multipanel drawings with generic titles like *A landscape vision* or *Landscape-Seascape*. The titles themselves speak of the new attitude to the subject. If, ten years earlier, one of his finest multipanel compositions had the title *Sixteen Studies on a Ceramic*

Richard Diebenkorn, 1922–1993
Ocean Park No. 83, 1975
Oil on canvas
100" × 81"
Collection: Corcoran Gallery of Art, Washington D.C.
Museum purchase, with aid of funds from the National Endowment for the Arts, William A Clark Fund and Mary M Hitchcock.

Theme, 1976, in this both identifying his point of departure for the inspiration as well as a point of entry for the viewer, and one of the major panels of the early eighties, *Metropolis I*, 1983–86, pointed to his fascination with the American cities and their freeways, bridges, skyscrapers and the various electrical structures, the new drawings related to far more abstract and general universal themes. The primary concern was with the "beautiful object", with calligraphy existing for its own sake. There is an intensity and spirituality in these works which saves them from being purely decorative and facile. It was Ruskin who commented that "All true landscape, whether simple or exalted, depends primarily for its interest on connection with humanity, or with spiritual powers."[38] In Blackburn's drawings of the later eighties, although some topographical references or starting points may exist, nothing is specific, it is a general spiritual evocation. The work can increasingly be related to meditative experiences or, as Peter Fuller commented on Blackburn's drawings, "the kind of illusion they encourage us to enter into is that upon which spiritual life, perhaps civilisation itself, depends".[39] The drawings have continued to draw praise from those who champion the spiritual tradition in art, like the British writer on the visual arts, the contemplative nun Sister Wendy Beckett.[40]

David Blackburn's first half dozen years in America were generally concerned with an urban environment in which the sense of geometry and design dominated. The quality of the mark was celebrated for its own sake. In their colour range, blues, purples and orange seem to predominate in these drawings, leading to a possible interpretation that there was a level on which they could be interpreted as an investigation into the qualities of neon light and the reflections of neon on buildings. By 1987 in the work there is a perceptible move away from the geometry which had governed the drawings for a number of years and an expression of a perceived need to describe the world, rather than simply alluding to it. This was accompanied by an introduction of a looser line and the investigation of pastoral landscapes, rather than of the urban environment. It was in 1987 that Blackburn travelled to Maine and executed a series of drawings which explored the

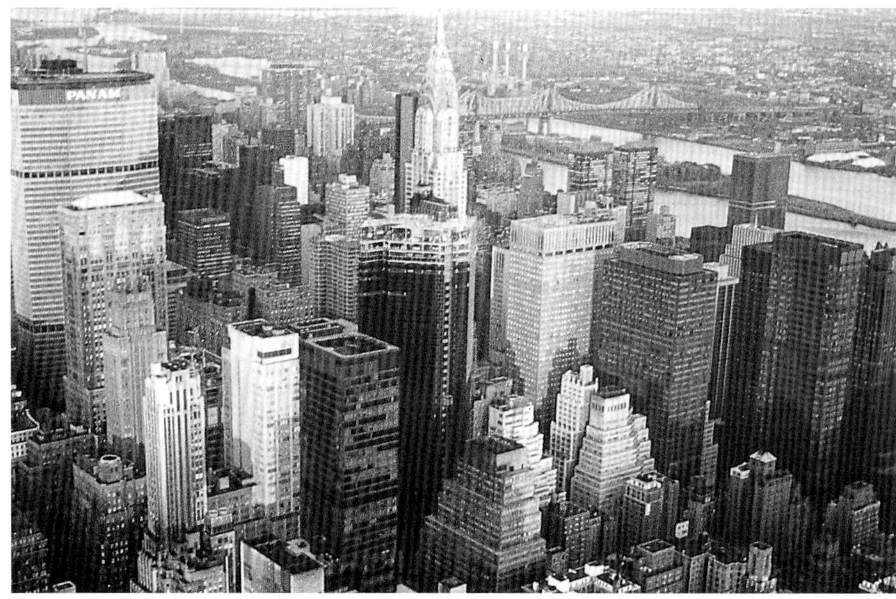

New York

surrounding landscape, and ventured into Canada particularly into the region round Lake Louise and the Canadian Rockies. Many of the drawings were in fact executed back in Yorkshire, but they explored the sense of blueness of the lakes, the quality of shimmering light and the idea of pine trees standing in the snow with a particular fascination with the effects of white. One of Blackburn's friends from Huddersfield, Lady Margaret Kagan, a perceptive, warm and highly cultured person, had settled in Boston and established for him a base which enabled him to work in north eastern America without seeking institutional affiliations.

Much of David Blackburn's earlier American work involved the idea of incorporating the notion of a window through which the viewer looks into the landscape. This was quite different from the Renaissance concept which the theorist Alberti termed "painting, as a window into the world". In the Renaissance context there was an implied break with earlier symbolic forms of representation and an expressed desire to create a convincing illusion of three-dimensional space within which figures and objects could be located. Blackburn's window was consciously conceived as an actual grid which lay on the surface of the work, with these lines sometimes alluding to telegraph wires and industrial structures. His window functioned as a sort of hologram, you could see through it and you could see behind it. You could see both the shallow space and the veils implying another dimension behind it. Towards the late eighties, particularly in a series of quite magical visionary seascapes, the window opened up into a series of veils, curtains or drifting mists, implying that these had somehow enveloped the landscape. The very high aerial vantage point adopted in many of these compositions, like those which could be related to flying over the Canadian cornfields and wheatfields, reduced the surface linear marks into something resembling musical notation. Crotchets, quavers and semiquavers, which may allude to bushes, trees, buildings or human forms, appear as if suspended dots on a musical score. It seems that as his compositions grew more abstract, the tighter became the formal structure which he adopted. When the references became more clearly representational, the looser the structure. Yet all of these developments occurred while working on the paper, rather than as preconceived devices. It is a similar process of work to that of Diebenkorn when he says "I begin the picture and wait for it to talk back to me".[41]

Collages occupy a peculiar place in David Blackburn's *oeuvre*. The earliest collages appeared in the seventies and they have continued to the present. Rarely more than a few are made in any given year and sometimes a couple of years will go by without a single collage. Although in one sense they constitute a fairly minor aspect of the artist's output, they do contain a number of absolutely brilliant works, which when better known, will be appreciated as significant pieces in collage art. Blackburn's collages almost inevitably appear at an end of a series of work, when there is a perceived need for a change in mood and approach. In the context of his work they play a subversive role, an abrupt break with whatever he is doing which could not be achieved in his process of continuous dialogue implicit in his pastel work. A number of his earlier collages did in fact reuse fragments of his own drawings which were incorporated into a totally new context, to give a startling and unexpected reading to the composition. In the eighties he increasingly drew on magazine images, which in the process of work would be totally stripped of any associative, representational quality and reinterpreted within the framework of a pastel drawing. Some exceptionally fine collages appeared with open spacious floating compositions — in a strange way reminiscent of Yves Tanguy's surrealist visions. Towards the close of the eighties and in the early nineties, Blackburn's collages have a stronger corporeal quality, alluding to Central Australian imagery and even figurative compositions. The tranquillity of some of the earlier collages is now superseded with a sense of dramatic, and at times even tragic, intensity. His collages do have this very wide range from the very simple elegant works with a primary interest in design, to quite elaborate compositions, playing with spatial ambiguities and areas of tonal, atmospheric pastel over which are suspended the collaged elements exhibiting their personalised torn edges.

The year 1989, in which David Blackburn turned fifty, formed a certain watershed in his life. A retrospective of his art was mounted by the Yale Center for British Art in New Haven in America. A large catalogue was published for the exhibition which contained a perceptive essay by the English critic Peter Fuller who argued that Blackburn was "one of the most original artists whose images are derived from landscape at work in Britain today".[42] In the same year two documentary films were devoted to his work[43] and the energetic gallery proprietors John and Katherine Hart became his dealers. Also by 1989, the health of his mother, then in her eighties, started to deteriorate as she suffered a series of minor strokes. His absences from Huddersfield became far less frequent and of very short duration.

David Blackburn has spent the early nineties living and working almost exclusively in Huddersfield. It has been a period of consolidation, with the expressed desire to concentrate on the making of "beautiful objects". His large panels such as *Landscape Vision No. 11*, 1992–3, have the quality of peace and lyricism, a sense of hidden poetry that one could associate with a Sung bowl or classical Chinese calligraphy. Despite the sophistication in the structure of his

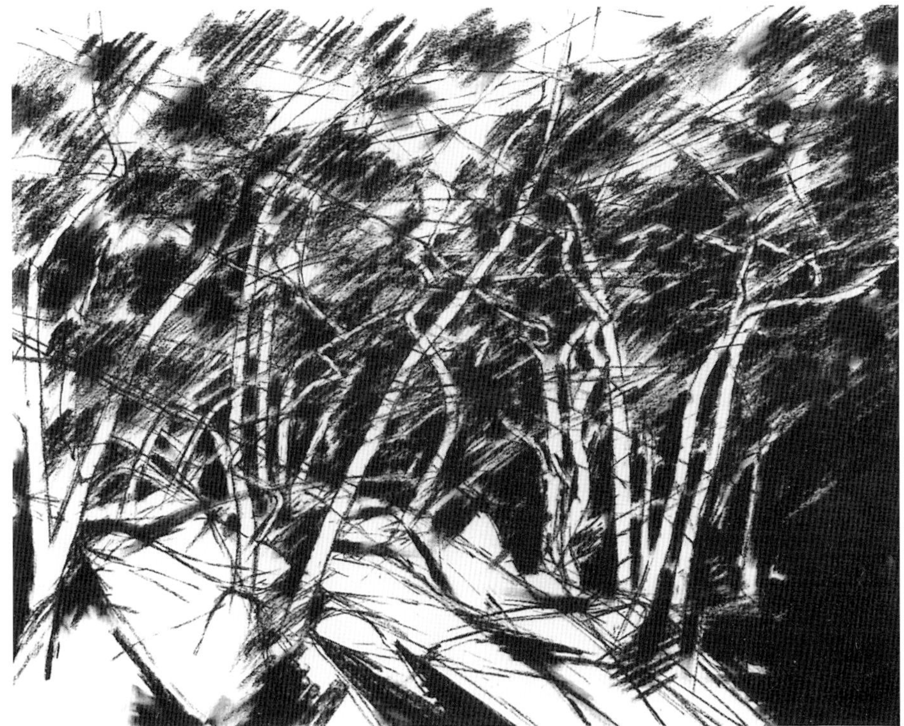

David Blackburn
Tree Study No. 1, 1978
Black Chalk
$23^1/_2" \times 19"$
Collection: John & Kit Hart

drawings of the nineties, there is an enormous ease and assuredness in the control of his medium as the nuances of white on white can bring to mind parallels with Malevich and Ryman. His drawings, with their endlessly ambiguous marks, strike within us certain chords which have a depth of resonance, as rich or as poor as the experiences which have informed our spiritual and artistic lives. Blackburn's unwillingness to compromise and hostility to easy eye-catching gimmicks have always guaranteed his work a well-informed and dedicated audience.

As an artist David Blackburn came of age in the early sixties when to many it seemed that modernism had run its course. The equation of modernism with newness by many of the art critics and gallery curators and the advent of Pop Art and the new figuration, suggested that a dead end had been reached. Post-Modernism conceptually opened the path for artists to glance backwards into art history, to reclaim those past traditions relevant to their practice and to use them as a rock on which to build their art. Unlike those who turned to Duchamp or the mainstream construct of Western European modernism, Blackburn chose to work within the tradition of the visionary landscape. It was a tradition which pointed back to Samuel Palmer and Blake, as well as Claude Lorraine and Friedrich and in

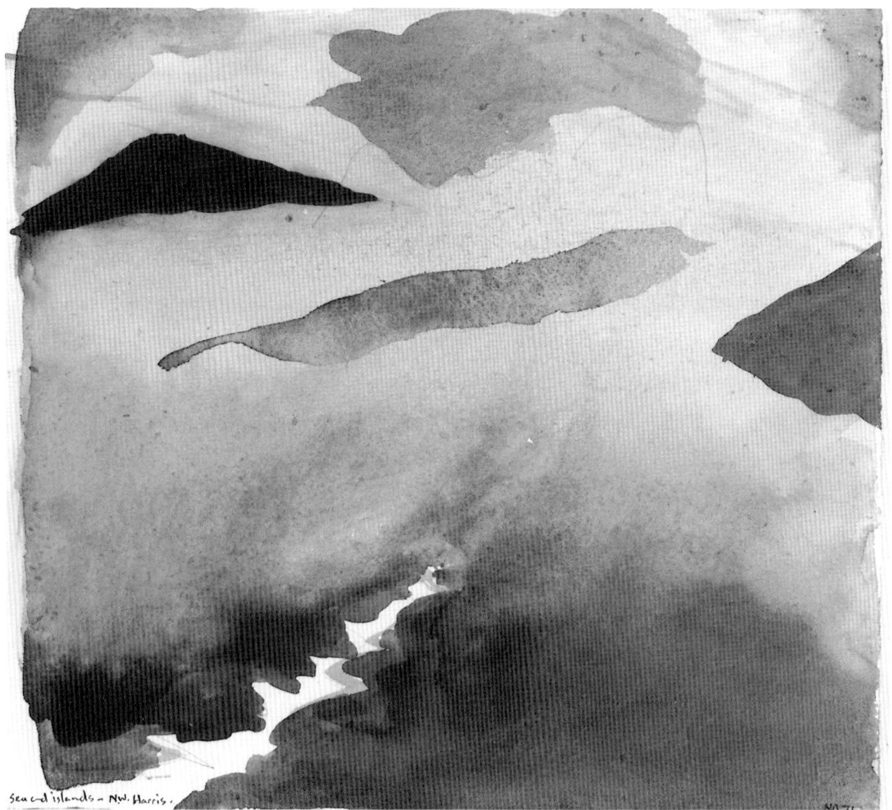

Norman Adams
Sea Bird Islands — North Harris, 1971
Watercolour
$10^1/_4$" × $11^1/_4$"
Private Collection

more contemporary practice to Sutherland and Nash, as well as Prunella Clough, Norman Adams, Fred Williams and Richard Diebenkorn. Working within a Post-Modernist context, Blackburn did not so much adopt a tradition, as adapt it to his own vision. For him the crucial factor remained the metaphysical transformation of the landscape into a metaphor which alluded to something beyond the ordinary and beyond the specific object. His work speaks of the need for art to be a spiritually intense experience, one with a quality of an internal harmony, a quietness and an ordering process. He made the deliberate decision that the neglected medium of the pastel had the qualities of fluidity and colour saturation through which he could best realise his vision, and proceeded to work exclusively in that medium for the next thirty years, except for rare excursions into collage.

While the ranking of artists is the prerogative of posterity rather than of contemporaries, David Blackburn has achieved in his work an art which is so uniquely his own and is of such haunting beauty and spiritual power that it has to be viewed as a major accomplishment on the international art scene.

References

1 Samuel Palmer, Letter to John Linnell, 21 December 1828, in Raymond Lister, editor, *The letters of Samuel Palmer*, vol. 1, Clarendon Press, Oxford 1974, pp. 47–52

2 Ibid., p. 49, cf. "That breathes on earth the air of paradise." William Wordsworth *From the Italian of Michelangelo.*

3 Mark Abley, editor, *The parting light: Selected writings of Samuel Palmer*, Carcanet, Manchester 1985, p. 7.

4 Douglas Cooper, *The work of Graham Sutherland*, David McKay, New York 1961, p. 7, cf. Roger Berthoud, *Graham Sutherland: A biography*, Faber, London 1982, pp. 52–54.

5 Ibid., p. 63.

6 Robert Rosenblum, *Modern painting and the Northern Romantic tradition: Friedrich to Rothko*, Thames and Hudson, London 1975.

7 David Blackburn, taped interview with the author, 16 January 1994.

8 For an account of life at the Huddersfield School of Art at the time see David Halliwell's play *Little Malcolm*, 1967.

9 David Blackburn, taped interview with the author, 16 January 1994.

10 Kenneth Clark, letter to David Blackburn, 9 May 1972.

11 Kenneth Clark, *Landscape into art*, Penguin, Harmondsworth 1956 (1949).

12 John Hayes, *The art of Graham Sutherland*, Phaidon, Oxford 1980, p. 27 ff.

13 David Blackburn, taped interview with the author, 22 June 1984.

14 Bernard Smith review, *Age* (Melbourne), 25 July 1965.

15 Kenneth Clark, *Landscape into art,* Penguin, Harmondsworth 1956, p. 142.

16 Between 1964 and 1965 he also made a number of etchings, aquatints, relief prints and lithographs. This was his only venture into printmaking.

17 Leonardo da Vinci, Human figure in a circle, illustrating proportion, pen and ink, Venice Academy, see A.E. Popham, *The drawings of Leonardo da Vinci,* Jonathan Cape, London 1946, plate 215.

18 Francis Bacon, *Three studies for figures at the base of a Crucifixion*, 1944, The Tate Gallery, London.

19 The idea for working in a triptych format Blackburn took from Pietro Lorenzetti's *Birth of the Virgin*, 1342, Museo dell'Opera del Duomo, Siena, which he saw in 1962.

20 David Blackburn, taped interview with the author, 17 January 1994.

21 On Thomas Watling and Joseph Lycett and their responses to the Australian landscape, see Bernard Smith, ed. *Documents on art and taste in Australia: The colonial period 1770–1914*, Oxford University Press, Melbourne 1975, pp. 8–17; 26–29.

22 *The Creation of Landscape,* 1971–75, 200 × 150 cm.

23 E.T. Cook and Alexander Wedderburn, eds., *The works of John Ruskin* (Modern Painters, vol. 3, pt iv), vol. 5, George Allen, London 1908, p. 367.

24 See, for example, his article "Rise and Fall of Romance" on David Blackburn's work in *The Age* (Melbourne), August 1973.

25 See Suzi Gablik, *Has modernism failed?* Thames and Hudson, London 1984; Rosalind E. Krauss, *The originality of the avant-garde and other modernist myths*, MIT, Cambridge MA 1986, pp. 161–70.

26 Quoted in Franco Solmi, *Morandi*, Rizzoli, New York 1988, p. 5; also see Lamberto Vitali, *Morandi: Catalogo generale*, 2nd edit., Electa, Milan 1983.

27 David Blackburn, taped interview with the author, 22 June 1984.

28 James Mollison, *A singular vision: The art of Fred Williams*, Australian National Gallery, Canberra 1989; Patrick McCaughey, *Fred Williams*, Bay Books, Sydney 1980.

29 David Blackburn visited Australia in 1963–66, 1971, 1973–74, 1977, 1978, 1980 and 1984.

30 David Blackburn, taped interview with the author, 17 August 1977.

31 Patrick McCaughey, catalogue introduction for exhibition at Joseph Brown Gallery, Melbourne 1973.

32 Russell Drysdale, letter to David Blackburn, 21 June 1972.

33 Typescript of speech by Lord Clark at the opening of *Drawings by David Blackburn* exhibition, York University, 13 October 1978. Most of it published in the *Yorkshire Post*, October 1978.

34 David Blackburn, taped interview with the author, 22 June 1984.

35 Andreas Franzke, *Tàpies*, Prestel, New York 1992, p. 7.

36 John Russell, *Richard Diebenkorn*, Marlborough Gallery catalogue, London 1973, p. 5.

37 Wallace Stevens quoted in John Elderfield, *The drawings of Richard Diebenkorn*, Museum of Modern Art, New York 1989, p. 59.

38 John Ruskin, *Modern Painters*, op. cit., vol. v, pt ix, p. 255.

39 Peter Fuller, catalogue essay, *David Blackburn: Light and landscape*, Yale Center for British Art, New Haven 1989, p. 13.

40 See, for example, her catalogue essay in *New work by David Blackburn*, Stein Bartlow Gallery, Chicago 1994.

41 Russell, *Richard Diebenkorn*, op. cit., p. 7.

42 Peter Fuller, catalogue essay in *David Blackburn: Light and landscape*, Yale Center for British Art, New Haven 1989, p. 7, reprinted in John MacDonald, ed., *Peter Fuller's Modern Painters*, London 1993.

43 BBC *Northern Lights*, programme and ITV *Celebrations* (30 minute documentary).

DAVID BLACKBURN
et la TRADITION DU PAYSAGE VISIONNAIRE

La préoccupation essentielle de David Blackburn, dans son oeuvre, ne consiste jamais à faire une transcription littérale, mais plutôt à représenter le paysage comme une métaphore visuelle, selon une tradition à laquelle appartiennent Samuel Palmer et Graham Sutherland. Dans ses premiers paysages visionnaires, Palmer transformait la réalité physique d'un paysage donné en une vision céleste.

Dans les années 20, Graham Sutherland s'inspira des premières oeuvres de Palmer. Pour lui, Palmer était le visionnaire serein dont l'immense force libératrice légitima le rejet de la restructuration de l'espace, prônée par le cubisme et le modernisme parisien alors en vogue. Robert Rosenblum proposa une autre interprétation de l'art moderne, mettant l'accent sur la tradition Romantique de l'Europe du Nord, où la spiritualité intuitive et les réactions émotionnelles à la nature semblaient plus adaptées que les valeurs purement formelles. Rosenblum présenta cette tradition artistique comme un continuum entre Friedrich et Blake et les Expressionnistes abstraits comme Gottlieb, Newman et Rothko, en passant par Van Gogh, Hodler, Munch, Kandinsky, Klee et Mondrian. Dans cette tradition de l'art moderne, les oeuvres de Palmer et de Sutherland occupent la place centrale. C'est dans cette tradition que s'inscrit l'oeuvre de David Blackburn.

David Blackburn naquit à Huddersfield en juin 1939. En 1959, il termina ses études à l'Ecole des Beaux-Arts de Huddersfield et obtint une bourse d'études au Royal College of Art de Londres. Depuis toujours, il était convaincu que l'art avait pour but de conférer aux phénomènes observables une signification transcendantale. Pour lui, l'art était la découverte de qualités magiques dans la réalité terrestre.

Son départ pour le Royal College of Art l'enleva à l'espace confiné du foyer pour le plonger dans l'immensité d'un environnement urbain. A Londres, il passait la majeure partie de son temps à contempler les grandes collections et à rechercher des objects qu'il ressentait comme magiques. Puis il revenait aux paysages du Yorkshire et à sa recherche d'images magiques, de langage et de formes, qui lui permettaient d'organiser les émotions éprouvées à Londres.

La personne qui eut le plus d'influence sur l'évolution artistique de Blackburn fut un autrichien, Gerhart Frankl, peintre émigré juif qui s'était installé à Londres, et qu'il rencontra en 1960. Frankl utilisait un mélange très efficace de pastel et de gouache pour obtenir des images aux couleurs détrempées, imprégnées d'une qualité évoquant d'autres univers. Ce fut l'influence de Frankl qui incita Blackburn à abandonner toutes les autres techniques et à travailler exclusivement au pastel.

En 1962, il rencontra Sir Kenneth Clark qui devint le principal protecteur et defenseur de son oeuvre. L'utilisation exclusive du pastel sur papier, dans la création de paysages visionnaires, n'était pas populaire à une période où la plupart des oeuvres réalisées à grande échelle étaient influencées par l'Ecole de New York. C'est le soutien de Clark qui lui apporta, à cette époque, l'assurance nécessaire pour poursuivre sa route sur la voie solitaire qu'il avait choisie.

Aprés avoir été diplômé du Royal College of Art en 1962, Blackburn entreprit un grand voyage afin de visiter les musées européens. Pendant cette période, son oeuvre semble s'inspirer surtout des maîtres de la Renaissance et du style gothique Allemand. Sa technique est dominée par l'attention qu'il porte aux signes créés par d'autres artistes, cherchant en eux un sens de l'histoire qui légitimerait, d'une certaine manière, sa propre méthode pour créer des signes.

A son retour, Blackburn accepta l'offre d'un poste à Melbourne, en Australie. Là-bas, le paysage qu'il rencontra lui était totalement étranger et lui posa un défi particulier. Ce paysage démesuré et sans relief lui donna le sentiment d'une redécouverte. Plus important encore, la principale tradition artistique australienne s'exprimait, pour diverses raisons historiques, dans la peinture de paysages qui, de ce fait, suscitait un grand intérêt.

Son premier voyage en Australie fut interrompu après trois années, lorsque son père tomba gravement malade. Toutefois, les oeuvres réalisées au cours de cette période expriment une certaine apogée des idées. Alors que de petits détails spécifiques tirés d'une observation immédiate sont mis en valeur, la métamorphose porte sur des images symboliques qui, à la manière d'un microcosme, évoquent les thèmes universels.

Blackburn a toujours travaillé sur des séries, le dernier tableau comportant des indices suggérant le début du prochain. Sa première série "Création" fut réalisée entre 1963 et 1966. Elle peut être interprétée à deux niveaux : un niveau littéral dans son contenu narratif et un niveau autobiographique révélé par l'obscurité croissante de vingt et un pastels à la pierre noire, pressentant la mort du père de l'artiste. L'imagerie est librement tirée d'une vaste tradition puisée dans les sources de l'histoire de l'art.

En 1966, Blackburn se lança dans une nouvelle série majeure de peintures, "Les Métamorphoses", où les transformations s'opèrent dans des espaces intérieurs suggérant l'enfermement. Toujours soucieux de laisser un message sur la condition humaine, il charge cette série de significations eschatologiques et autobiographiques. Celle-ci peut sans doute être considérée comme un grand tournant, ses études organiques précédentes étant abandonnées au profit de structures picturales plus complexes et plus riches. Pour la première fois, la couleur joue un rôle plus décisif.

Outre l'introduction de la couleur, sa nouvelle méthode de travail comporte une subtile évolution dans le développement de la technique. Il commence à utiliser un papier plus résistant, au grain plus épais, et tend à couvrir la surface entière d'une couche de pastel de couleur. Sur cette base fluide, il applique d'autre couches de pastel. Ce procédé, dans sa conception, comporte de nombreux points communs avec celui qu'emploient les Expressionistes abstraits. La surface du travail peut être considérée comme une arène dans laquelle l'artiste affronte son moyen d'expression et les résultats de cette rencontre transparaissent dans le tableau terminé.

En 1971, Blackburn retourna en Australie comme conférencier associé à l'Université de Melbourne. Il s'aperçut que, lors de sa première visite, il n'avait rien compris au paysgae australien. Il voyagea alors dans les terres rouges de l'intérieur du pays à la recherche d'un répertoire d'images plus riches, qui devaient imprégner son oeuvre pendant les dix années suivantes.

Blackburn entreprit ce qui allait devenir l'une de ses plus importantes réalisations dans la tradition du paysage visionnaire, sa série "Création de Paysage" exécutée entre 1971 et 1975. Cette oeuvre intègre deux sources importantes d'innovation : la découverte du lourd papier Arches qui s'imbibe littéralement de pastel pour produire un rayonnement interne lumineux, ainsi que la rencontre avec la tradition russo-byzantine des icônes hagiographiques, où le Saint au centre de l'icône est entouré par toute une série de scènes narratives évoquant des épisodes de sa vie. Dans le grand panneau "Création de Paysage", quatre grandes peintures, étroitement reliées, forment une image centrale, autour de laquelle seize peintures plus petites imposent un récit symbolique.

Au début des années 70, les critiques britanniques et australiens reconnaissent à Blackburn le statut d'artiste. En dépit de leurs éloges, son oeuvre ne déclenche pas un engouement international. Ceci trouve probablement son explication d'une part, dans les préjugés des principaux conservateurs artistiques occidentaux contre la technique du pastel sur papier, et d'autre part, dans l'obstination de Blackburn à s'inscrire dans une tradition qui le faisait paraître comme allant à contre-courant du modernisme alors en vogue. La puissance artistique de Blackburn réside précisément dans le fait qu'il a choisi d'être un innovateur au sein d'une grande tradition de l'histoire de l'art, la tradition du paysage visionnaire personnel.

L'approche selon laquelle l'art serait une chronique, populaire dans l'art contemporain, est généralement associée au concept de l'art en tant qu'autobiographie. La conception blackburnienne de l'art en tant que chronique est proche de celle de Morandi, où les toiles sont imprégnées d'un contenu émotionnel très personnel. Chacune des oeuvres est autonome, mais lorsqu'elle est examinée dans l'ensemble de la série, elle montre une progression et une intensité spirituelle croissante. Cette approche montre qu'il existe, dans les toiles de Blackburn, un paysage métaphysique intérieur.

L'expérience authentique vécue en Australie transparaît dans la nouvelle gamme de couleurs que Blackburn, sous l'influence des couleurs de l'intérieur du pays, utilise. La vision du paysage par Fred Williams, artiste australien, l'influença peut-être plus formellement encore. Blackburn s'aperçut, au fur et à mesure que son appréciation du paysage se développait, à quel point l'oeuvre de Williams s'harmonisait avec les particularités uniques du paysage australien. Williams aplatissait structurellement l'espace pictural et réduisait la végétation à des pavés de couleurs extrèmement expressifs, qui semblaient suspendus à la surface plutôt qu'ancrés dans le paysage. Tout au long des années 70, la vision de Williams ainsi que ses signes furent des facteurs importants dans l'oeuvre de Blackburn. Ce fut pour lui une période artistiquement étrange, car il s'identifia de plus en plus comme un artiste australien, en partie pour répondre à ce sentiment d'aliénation dont il avait fait l'expérience au sein du monde artistique britannique.

Le point culminant de son oeuvre au cours des années 70 fut une exposition à l'Université de York en 1978, ouverte par Lord Clark. Dans son discours d'ouverture, Clark interpréta Blackburn comme ce-solitaire qui travaille en marge des conventions artistiques alors admises en Grande-Bretagne, comme une personne travaillant exclusivement à partir de sa vision intérieure et se distinguant de toutes les traditions. Le fait d'être perçu comme tel par l'un des historiens artistiques les mieux informés de l'époque est en soi très significatif. La tradition du paysage visionnaire était soit négligée, soit considérée comme obsolète, si bien qu'aucune relation ne fut établie entre celle-ci et l'oeuvre de Blackburn.

A measure que la santé de sa mère s'aggravait, il devint de plus en plus difficile à Blackburn de s'absenter longtemps de Londres. Comparée à l'Australie, l'Amérique du Nord semblait très proche. Pendant les dix années qui suivirent, il se rendit fréquemment en Amérique et au Canada. Ses paysages américains des années 80 font référence à la topographie urbaine. Ils présentent des qualités sur le plan architectural, mais sa préoccupation première, la description d'un monde qu'il observe, a disparu au profit d'allusions à toutes sortes d'associations. Ses toiles ont presque totalement perdu leur spécificité.

Le peintre américain Diebenkorn, et plus particulièrement ses toiles "Ocean Park", furent pour Blackburn une décourverte essentielle. Il existe un certain parallèle entre le traitement du paysage de Blackburn et de Diebenkorn ; tous deux utilisent des abstractions réductrices, non figuratives; tous deux manifestent un intérêt pour le formalisme et le structuralisme, et adhèrent d'une manière générale aux théories picturales des Expressionnistes abstraits. Tous deux utilisent des symboles très chargés émotionellment et de riches métaphores. Les deux leçons les plus importantes que Blackburn tira de Diebenkorn furent la relation entre la ligne et le champ tonal, et le sens du paysage descriptif, qui est, dans une grande mesure, indépendant d'un lieu spécifique.

Depuis le milieu des années 80 jusqu'au début des années 90 apparâit une série de peintures monumentales, à panneaux multiples, dont les titres génériques comme "Vision du paysage" indiquent une nécessité d'analyser ce sujet. Les toiles de Blackburn réalisées à la fin des années 80 n'indiquent rien de précis, à l'exception de quelques références topographiques ou quelques points de départ. C'est une évocation spirituelle globale. L'oeuvre se rapproche de plus en plus des expériences de méditation.

Le Yale Center for British Art, à New Haven, en Amérique organisa en 1989 une exposition de l'oeuvre de Blackburn. Un catalogue fut publié, comportant un essai perspicace écrit par l'ancien critique d'art Peter Fuller, selon lequel Blackburn était l'un des artistes les plus originaux travaillant en Grande-Bretagne aujourd'hui. La même année, deux films documentaires furent consacrés à son oeuvre et les propriétaires dynamiques de la galerie, John et Katherine Hart, devinrent ses agents. Au début des années 90, il travaillait exclusivement à Huddersfield, période de consolidation pendant laquelle il exprimait un désir de s'investir dans la fabrication de "beaux objets".

Bien que la classification des artistes soit la prérogative de la postérité plutôt que celle de l'époque contemporaine, l'oeuvre de David Blackburn exprime un art qui lui est si uniquement personnel, qui est d'une telle puissance spirituelle et d'une beauté si obsédante, qu'il doit être considéré comme un accomplissement majeur sur la scène internationale de l'art.

DAVID BLACKBURN
und die TRADITION DER VISIONÄREN LANDSCHAFT

Im Vordergrund des Schaffens von David Blackburn steht nicht die fotografische Darstellung der Landschaft sondern die Landschaft als sichtbarer bildlicher Ausdruck. Dieser Tradition gehören auch Samuel Palmer und Graham Sutherland an. Die frühen visionären Landschaften von Samuel Palmer haben die physische Realität einer spezifischen Landschaft zu einer himmlischen Vision verwandelt.

In den 20er Jahren haben Palmers frühe Werke auch Graham Sutherland inspiriert. Für ihn war Palmer der ruhige Visionär, der mit einer großen, befreienden Kraft die Ablehnung des Pariser Standardmodernismus und der Kubistischen Neustrukturierung des Raums legitimierte. Robert Rosenblum hatte eine alternative Interpretation der Modernen Kunst vorgebracht. Im Mittelpunkt stand die nordeuropäische Tradition der Romantik, die mit intuitiver Geistigkeit und einer gefühlsgeprägten Reaktion der Natur mehr Relevanz als den rein formalen Werten zumaß. Rosenblum verfolgte diese Kunsttradition als ununterbrochene Reihe von Friedrich und Blake über Van Gogh, Hodler, Munch, Kandinsky, Klee und Mondrian bis zu den abstrakten Expressionisten wie Gottlieb, Newman und Rothko. In dieser Tradition der Modernen Kunst nehmen die Werke von Palmer und Sutherland einen zentralen Platz ein. Dieser Tradition gehört auch das Werk von David Blackburn an.

David Blackburn wurde im Juni 1939 in Huddersfield geboren. 1959 absolvierte er sein Studium an der Huddersfield School of Art und erhielt ein Stipendium für das Royal College of Art in London. Er war immer der Überzeugung, daß es ein Ziel der Kunst ist, der wahrnehmbaren Erscheinung eine abstrakte Bedeutung zu verleihen. Für ihn war Kunst die Entdeckung magischer Eigenschaften innerhalb der banalen Wirklichkeit.

Sein Wechsel zum Royal College of Art versetzte ihn aus der Enge seiner Heimat in die Weite der Großstadt. In London beschäftigte er sich intensiv mit den großen Kunstsammlungen und suchte Gegenstände, die für ihn eine magische Bedeutung hatten. Er kehrte anschließend nach Yorkshire zurück, um seine Eindrücke aus London zu ordnen.

Der jüdische Maler Gerhart Frankl, der sich nach seiner Auswanderung aus Österreich in London niedergelassen hatte, übte den größten Einfluß auf die künstlerische Entwicklung David Blackburns aus. Mit einer wirkungsvollen Mischung von Pastellfarben und Gouache hat Frankl farbgesättigte Bilder, die mit einer gewissen Weltferne erfüllt waren, geschaffen. Es war der Einfluß Frankls, der Blackburn dazu bewegte, ausschließlich mit Pastellfarben zu arbeiten.

1962 lernte Blackburn Sir Kenneth Clark kennen, der sich für ihn einsetzte und zu seinem großen Förderer wurde. Blackburns ausschließliche Verwendung von Pastellfarbe auf Papier für die Schaffung von visionären Landschaften erfreute sich weniger Beliebtheit, da die meisten Werke von der New York School beeinflußt und übergroß dimensioniert waren.

Clarks Unterstützung gab ihm aber das Selbstvertrauen den selbst ausgesuchten Weg als Einzelgänger weiter zu verfolgen.

Nach der Graduation an dem Royal College of Art im Jahre 1962 unternahm Blackburn eine längere Tour durch die Museen Europas. In dieser Phase hatten die deutschen Meister der Gothik und Renaissance die größte Bedeutung für sein Werk. Es ist typisch für seine Arbeitsmethode, daß er sich die Merkmale anderer Künstler genau ansah, auf der Suche nach einem Sinn für die Stilrichtung, der den Aufbau seiner eigenen Merkmale irgendwie legitimieren würde.

Nach seiner Rückkehr nahm Blackburn eine Stelle in Melbourne, Australien, an. Hier fand er eine Landschaft vor, die ihm völlig unbekannt war und für ihn eine besondere Herausforderung darstellte. Er hatte das Gefühl, daß er wegen der riesigen Ausmaße und Flachheit die Landschaft neu entdeckte. Noch bedeutender war die Tatsache, daß aus historischen Gründen die Landschaftsmalerei eine Haupttradition der australischen Kunst war und sehr ernst genommen wurde.

Sein erster Australienaufenthalt wurde von der schweren Krankheit seines Vaters unterbrochen. Wenn man seine Werke dieser Periode betrachtet, sieht man ein gewisses Zusammenkommen von verschiedenen Ideen. Obwohl kleine, spezifische Details aus der eigenen Erfahrung im Mittelpunkt standen, wurden sie in eine Bildersymbolik verwandelt, die im mikrokosmischen Sinne universelle Themen darstellte.

Blackburn arbeitet immer in Serien, wobei die letzte Zeichnung auf den Anfang der nächsten hinweist. Seine erste Serie "Schöpfung" schuf er zwischen 1963 und 1966, mit einem erzählerischen Inhalt. Man kann sie auch als Autobiographie betrachten, wobei die zunehmende Dunkelheit der 21 Zeichnungen in schwarzer Kreide als Vorahnung des Todes seines Vaters interpretiert werden kann. Die Bildersymbolik stützt sich auf eine breite Tradition kunsthistorischer Quellen.

Blackburn begann 1966 eine große neue Serie, "Die Metamorphosen". Diese Serie beschäftigt sich mit Verwandlungen innerhalb innerer Räume, die etwas Eingeschlossenes an sich haben. Es war für ihn wichtig, den Zustand der Menschheit zu kommentieren. Die Serie ist reich an philosophischer und autobiographischer Bedeutung. Sie könnte man als Wendepunkt betrachten, da viel komplexere Bildstrukturen seine früheren organischen Studien ersetzten und zum ersten Mal Farbe eine entscheidende Rolle spielte.

Zusätzlich zur Verwendung von Farbe zeigte sein Werk eine subtile neue Entwicklung. Er begann mit schwererem, strukturiertem Papier zu arbeiten. Blackburn bedeckte die ganze Oberfläche mit einer Schicht Pastellfarbe. Auf diese Schicht wurden weitere Pastellschichten aufgetragen. Diese Arbeitsweise hatte konzeptionell viel mit den Methoden der abstrakten Expressionisten gemeinsam. Die Arbeitsfläche konnte man als Arena betrachten, in der der Künstler seinem Medium begegnete. Das Ergebnis dieser Begegnung bleibt im endgültigen Werk festgehalten.

1971 kehrte Blackburn als Gastdozent an die Universität Melbourne zurück. Es wurde ihm klar, daß er bei seinem ersten Besuch die australische Landschaft kaum verstanden hatte. Bei diesem Besuch reiste er ins rote Innnere des Landes, auf der Suche nach einer reichen Bildersymbolik, die sein Werk im nächsten Jahrzehnt prägte.

Blackburn realisierte mit seiner Serie "Schaffung einer Landschaft", die zwischen 1971 und 1975 entstand, eines seiner wichtigsten Werke in der Tradition der visionären Landschaft. In dieser Serie wurden zwei Innovationsquellen integriert. Die Entdeckung des schweren "Arches Papiers", das die Pastellfarbe buchstäblich aufsaugt und eine leuchtende innere Glut erzeugt, und die Begegnung mit der russisch-byzantinischen Tradition der Ikonenmalerei. Der Heilige ist in der Mitte der Ikone von einer Reihe von Szenen umgeben, die Episoden seines Lebens darstellen. Das große Tafelbild "Schaffung einer Landschaft" verbindet vier große Zeichnungen in einem zentralen Bild, um das 16 kleinere Zeichnungen eine symbolische Erzählung gestalten.

In den frühen 70er Jahren hatte sich der künstler Blackburn unter den britischen und australischen Kritikern etabliert. Trotz des kritischen Lobes wurde sein Werk international noch nicht bekannt. Die Erklärung hierfür lag wahrscheinlich darin, daß die einflußreichen Leiter der westlichen Kunstsammlungen gegen Pastellfarbe auf Papier als Medium voreingenommen waren und daß Blackburn's Stil den Eindruck vermittelte, daß er sich in entgegengesetzter Richtung zur Hauptbewegung des Modernismus bewegte. Die Kraft seiner Kunst lag aber gerade in seiner Entscheidung, als Neuerer innerhalb einer großen Kunsttraditon, der persönlichen visionären Landschaft, zu arbeiten.

Das in der Modernen Kunst beliebte Tagebuchkonzept wird normalerweise mit dem Konzept der Kunst als Autobiographie identifiziert. Die Idee von Kunst als Tagebuch hat bei Blackburn eine Ähnlichkeit mit dem Werk von Morandi, bei dem die Zeichnungen von sehr persönlichen Gefühlen geprägt sind. Jedes Werk ist autonom, aber wenn man das Ganze als Serie betrachtet, entdeckt man eine allmähliche Progression und eine zunehmende geistige Intensität. Diese künstlerische Einstellung bedeutet, daß in den Zeichnungen von Blackburn eine innere metaphysische Landschaft gegenwärtig ist.

Der Einfluß Australiens machte sich in der neuen, von Blackburn eingesetzten Farbpalette, die von den Farben des Landesinneren geprägt war, bemerkbar. Noch wichtiger war der formelle Einfluß der Landschaftsvisionen des australischen Künstlers Fred Williams. Während Blackburn die australische Landschaft immer mehr zu schätzen lernte, wurde ihm klar, wie das Werk Williams den einmaligen Eigenschaften der australischen Landschaft getreu wurde. Williams hatte die Struktur des Bildraumes abgeflacht und die Vegetation auf ausdrucksvolle Farbformen reduziert. Die Farbformen schwebten über die Bildoberfläche anstatt in der Landschaft verankert zu sein. In den ganzen 70er Jahren stellten die Visionen und die stilistischen Eigenschaften der Bilder von Williams einen wichtigen Faktor im Werk von Blackburn dar. Es war ein seltsames Jahrzehnt für seine Kunst, weil Blackburn sich zunehmend als australischer Künstler betrachtete. Dies war zum Teil eine Reaktion auf das Gefühl der Entfremdung, das er in der britischen Kunstwelt empfand.

Der Höhepunkt seines Schaffens in den 70er Jahren war eine Ausstellung in der Universität von York, die von Lord Clark eröffnet wurde. Clark interpretierte in seiner Eröffnungsrede das Werk Blackburns als das eines Einzelgängers, der außerhalb der herkömmlichen britischen Kunstbewegung seiner Zeit und unabhängig von allen Traditionen ausschließlich nach einer inneren Vision arbeitete. Das einer der bestinformierten Kunsthistoriker seiner Zeit Blackburn so gesehen hatte, ist an sich von großer Bedeutung, da die Tradition der visionären Landschaft entweder so vernachlässigt oder so veraltet war, daß man sie nicht mit dem Werk von Blackburn in Verbindung gebracht hätte.

Die Krankheit seiner Mutter machte es Blackburn immer schwieriger, längere Zeit von England fortzubleiben. Im Vergleich zu Australien war Nordamerika relativ nah. In den nächsten 10 Jahren unternahm er daher mehrere Reisen nach Amerika und Kanada. Dort zeichnete er Stadtlandschaften. Eine Eigenschaft dieser Landschaften ist ihre architektonische Struktur. Diese Bilder haben aber nicht das Ziel, die wahrnehmbare Welt zu beschreiben. Es sind Anspielungen auf Assoziationen aller Art, wobei das Konkrete fast völlig untergegangen ist. Eine große Entdeckung für Blackburn war der amerikanische Maler Diebenkorn mit seinen "Ocean Park" Bildern. Es besteht eine gewisse Ähnlichkeit zwischen seiner Behandlung der Landschaft und dem Werk Blackburns: Beide verwenden reduktive, nicht objektive Abstraktionen unter Berücksichtigung der Theorien des Strukturalismus und des Formalismus und halten sich allgemein an die Konzepte des Abstrakten Expressionismus. Das Werk beider Künstler ist von emotionsgeladenen Symbolen und reichen Metaphern geprägt. Die zwei wichtigsten Lehren, die Blackburn den Bildern Diebenkorns entnahm, waren das Verhältnis zwischen Linie und Klang der Farben und der Sinn für eine Landschaft, die weitgehend unabhängig von einem bestimmten Ort ist. Ende der 80er Jahre entstand eine Reihe riesiger Tafelbilder mit dem Titel "Landschaftsvision". In den Zeichnungen der späten 80er Jahre sieht man zwar einige topographische Andeutungen und Ansatzpunkte, aber nichts Konkretes. Sie sind eine allgemeine geistige Heraufbeschwörung und Können zunehmend mit Meditationserlebnissen in Verbindung gebracht werden.

1989 hat das Yale Center für britische Kunst New Haven, USA, eine Ausstellung mit Blackburns Werken organisiert. Der Katalog der Ausstellung enthält einen einsichtigen Essay des verstorbenen Kritikers Peter Fuller, der schreibt, daß Blackburn derzeit einer der originellsten Künstler Großbritanniens sei. Im selben Jahr wurden zwei Dokumentarfilme seinem Werk gewidmet. Die engagierten Galeriebesitzer John und Katherine Hart wurden zu seinen Kunsthändlern. In den frühen 90er Jahren arbeitete er ausschließlich in Huddersfield, in einer Phase der Konsolidierung, in der er sich mit der Schaffung von "schönen Gegenständen" beschäftigte.

Obwohl die Einordnung von Künstlern das Vorrecht der Nachwelt und nicht das der Zeitgenossen ist, hat David Blackburn mit seinem Werk eine Kunst geschaffen, die ganz deutlich seine eigene ist und darüber hinaus von einer derartigen eindringlichen Schönheit und geistiger Kraft geprägt ist, daß man ihre Bedeutung in der internationalen Kunstwelt als sehr groß beurteilen muß.

List of Colour Plates
Planchesdecouleur
Farbbilder

p. 68
Aerial Freeway, 1984.
Autoroute Aerienne.
Aeriel Freeway.
Pastel. 23 1/2" × 20 1/2". Private Collection.

p. 69
Metropolis I, 1983–86.
Metropolis 1.
Metropole 1.
Pastel. 73" × 58 1/2".

p. 70
Window — Architectural II, 1986.
Fenêtre, Motif Architectural 2.
Fensterarchitektonik 2.
Pastel. 24 1/2" × 21". Private Collection.

p. 71
Landscape Vision No. 1, 1986.
Vision du Paysage Numero 1.
Vision einer Landschaft Nr. 1.
Pastel. 60" × 65" (Polyptych, 15 pieces). Private Collection.

p. 72
Mountain with Road — Banff, 1987.
Route dans la Montagne, Banff.
Berg mit Straße, Banff.
Pastel. 16" × 13 1/2". Private Collection.

p. 73
Landscape Vision No. 3, 1988.
Vision du Paysage Numero 3.
Vision einer Landschaft Nr. 3.
Pastel. 60" × 65". Private Collection.

p. 74
A Mystical View of the Sea, 1988.
Une Vue Mystique de la Mer.
Mystischer Meeresblick.
Pastel. 21" × 25 1/2". Private Collection.

p. 75
Lake Landscape — Alberta, 1987.
Paysage de Lac, Alberta.
Seelandschaft, Alberta.
Pastel. 25 1/2" × 21". Collection: Yale Center for British Art.

p. 76
Blue Moorland II, 1989.
Lande Bleue 2.
Blaues Heideland.
Pastel. 14 1/4" × 11 1/2". Private Collection.

p. 77
Sunlit Moorland with Wall, 1989.
Lande Ensoleillee avec Mur.
Sonniges Heideland mit Mauer.
Pastel. 14 1/4" × 11 1/2". Private Collection.

p. 78
Evening Landscape with Black Wall, 1989.
Paysage Vespéral et Mur Noir.
Abendlandschaft mit schwarzer Mauer.
Pastel. 14 1/4" × 17". Private Collection.

p. 79
Cliff Seascape, 1989.
Paysage Marin et Falaises.
Meereslandschaft mit Klippen.
Pastel. 17" × 14 1/4". Private Collection.

p. 80
Two Stones and Hillside — Evening, 1990.
Deux Rochers et Coteau, Soir.
Zwei Steine und Hang, Abend.
Pastel. 16" × 13 1/2". Private Collection.

p. 81
A Landscape Vision No. 7, 1990.
Une Vision du Paysage Numero 7.
Vision einer Landschaft Nr. 7.
Pastel. 60" × 65". Private Collection.

p. 82
Sunlit Landscape — Peak District, 1991.
Paysage Ensoleille, Peak District.
Sonnige Landschaft, Peak District.
Pastel. 25 1/2" × 21". Private Collection.

p. 83
Sunlit Landscape, 1990.
Paysage Ensoleille.
Sonnige Landschaft.
Pastel. 17" × 14 1/2". Private Collection.

p. 84
Tree Study — Pale Sunlight, 1990.
Etude D'Arbres, Soleil Pale.
Studie eines Baumes; blaßes Sonnenlicht.
Pastel. 25" × 19". Private Collection.

p. 85
Winter Window, 1991.
Fenêtre sur L'Hiver.
Winterfenster.
Pastel. 21" × 25". Private Collection.

p. 86.
Cooling Towers No. 3, 1991.
Tours de Refroidissement Numero 3.
Kühltürme Nr. 3.
Pastel. 25" × 21". Private Collection.

p. 87.
Industrial Shipyard, 1992.
Chantier Naval Industriel.
Industrielle Werft.
Pastel. 25" × 19". Private Collection.

p. 88
Landscape — Edale, 1990.
Paysage, Edale.
Landschaft in Edale.
Pastel. 16" × 13 1/2". Private Collection.

p. 89
Landscape Vision No. 10, 1991–92.
Vision du Paysage Numero 10.
Vision einer Landschaft Nr. 10.
Pastel. 63" × 69". Private Collection.

p. 90
Study, 1992.
Etude.
Studie.
Pastel & Collage. 17" × 15". Private Collection.

p. 91
Figurative collage, 1992.
Collage Figuratif.
Gegenständliche Collage.
Pastel & Collage. 16" × 14".

p. 92
Japanese Tree II, 1993.
Arbre Japonais Numero 2.
Japanischer Baum Nr. 2.
Pastel. 24" × 19". Private Collection.

p. 93
Landscape Vision No. 11, 1992–93.
Vision du Paysage Numero 11.
Vision einer Landschaft Nr. 11.
Pastel. 64" × 70". Private Collection.

p. 94
Woodland Window, 1993.
Fenêtre sur la Forêt.
Waldfenster.
Pastel. 20" × 24". Private Collection.

p. 95
Beach Window, 1993.
Fenêtre sur la Plage.
Strandfenster.
Pastel. 21" × 25". Private Collection.

p. 96
White Collage, 1993.
Collage Blanc.
Weiße Collage.
Pastel & Collage. 17" × 15".

p. 97
Cliff Blue, 1993.
Falaise, Bleu.
Klippe blau.
Pastel & Collage. 15" × 17".

p. 98
Sunset Wheatfields, 1993.
Champs de Ble au Couchant.
Weizenfelder bei Sonnenuntergang.
Pastel. 14 1/2" × 16". Private Collection.

p. 99
Blue and Orange, 1993.
Bleu et Orange.
Blau und Orange.
Pastel. 25" × 21". Private Collection.

p. 100
Stones and Sunset, 1993.
Rochers et Soleil Couchant.
Steine und Sonnenuntergang.
Pastel. 14 1/4" × 17". Private Collection.

p. 101
Stones and Canadian Wheatfields, 1993.
Rochers et Champs de Ble Canadiens.
Steine und kanadische Weizenfelder.
Pastel. 24" × 20". Private Collection.

p. 102
Mystic Stone, 1993.
Rocher Mystique.
Mystischer Stein.
Pastel. 24" × 20". Private Collection.

p. 103
Winter Stones, 1993.
Rochers en Hiver.
Wintersteine.
Pastel. 25" × 21". Private Collection.

p. 104
Mystical Tree (study for Landscape Vision No. 14), 1994.
Arbre Mystique.
Mystischer Baum.
Pastel. 17" × 14 1/4" (panel 2).

p. 105
Dark Pool — Sunset, 1994.
Etang Sombre au Couchant.
Sonnenuntergang am dunklen Teich.
Pastel. 24" × 20". Private Collection.

p. 106
Two Stones and Sunburst, 1994.
Deux Rochers et Échappée de Soleil.
Zwei Steine und plötzlicher Sonnenschein.
Pastel. 24 3/4" × 20".

p. 107
Landscape Vision No. 13, 1993.
Vision du Paysage Numero 13.
Vision einer Landschaft Nr. 13.
Pastel. 65" × 70".

p. 108
Three Stones, 1993.
Trois Rochers.
Drei Steine.
Pastel. 16" × 14 1/2". Private Collection.

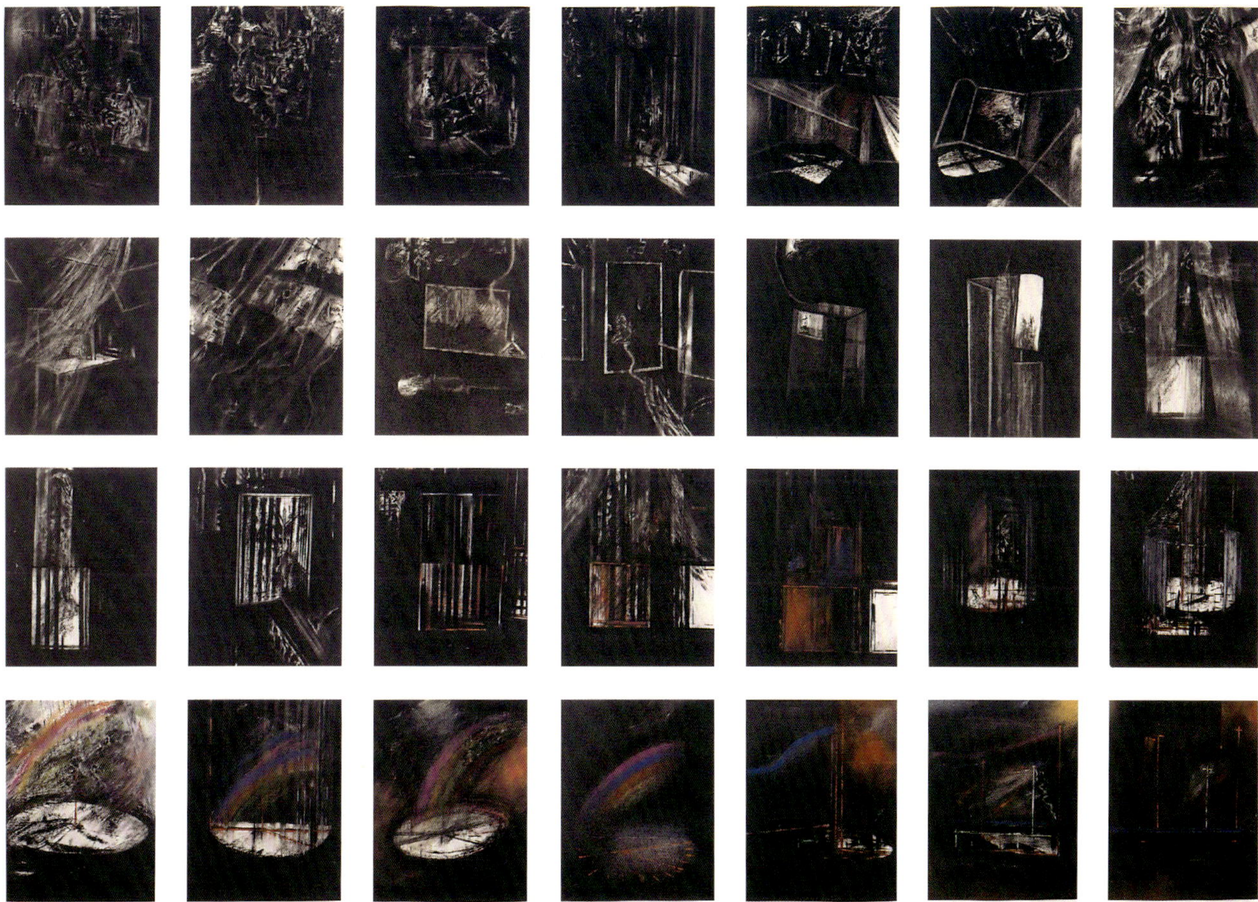

The Metamorphoses Series, 1967-68
Pastel
70" × 93 1/2"
individually 12 3/4" × 10 1/4"
Collection: The Artist

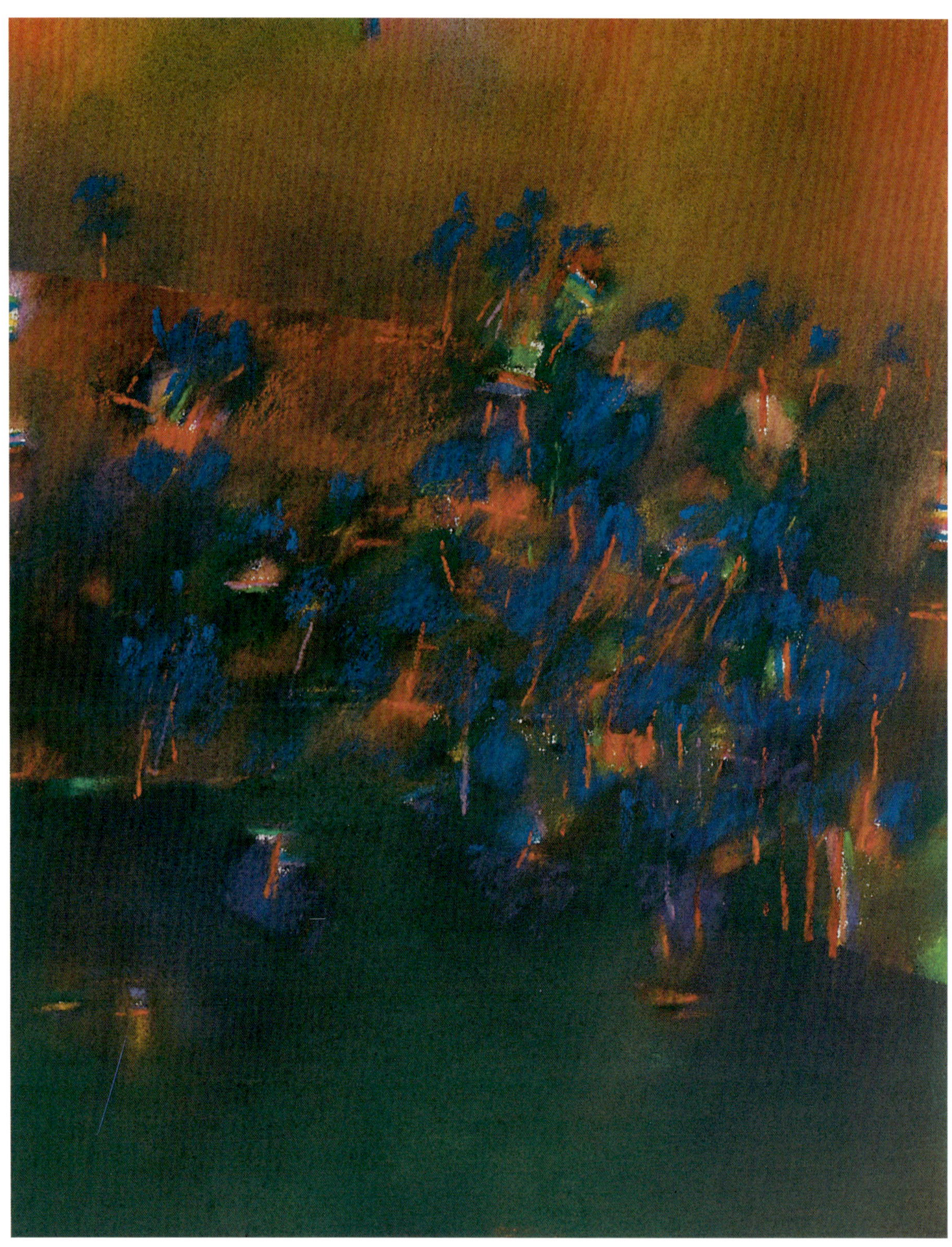

Gum Trees and Pool, Belgrave, 1971
Pastel
15" × 11½"
Private Collection

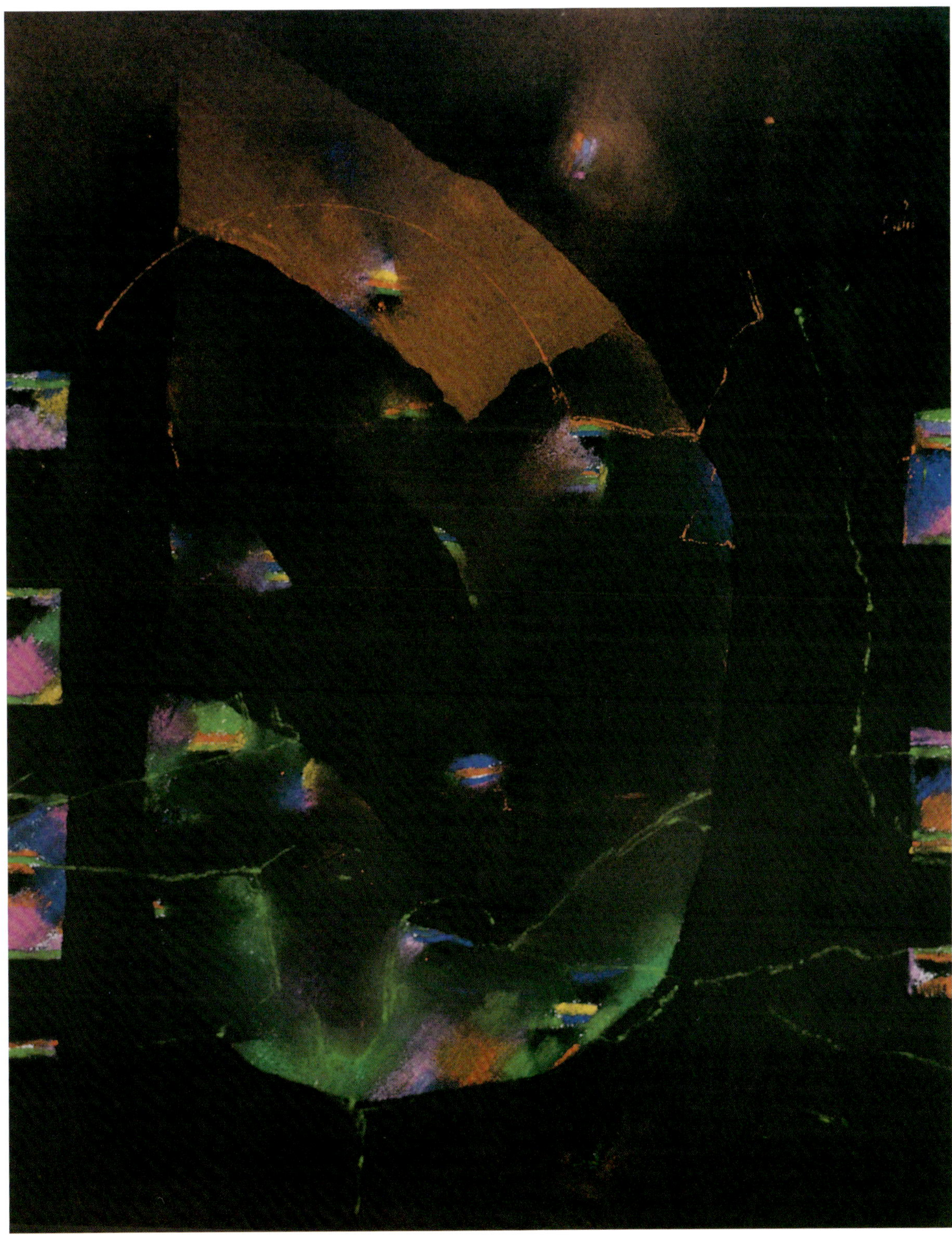

Detail from Landscape Variations (panel of 25), 1978–80
Pastel
81" × 69"
Individually 15" × 11 1/2"
Private Collection

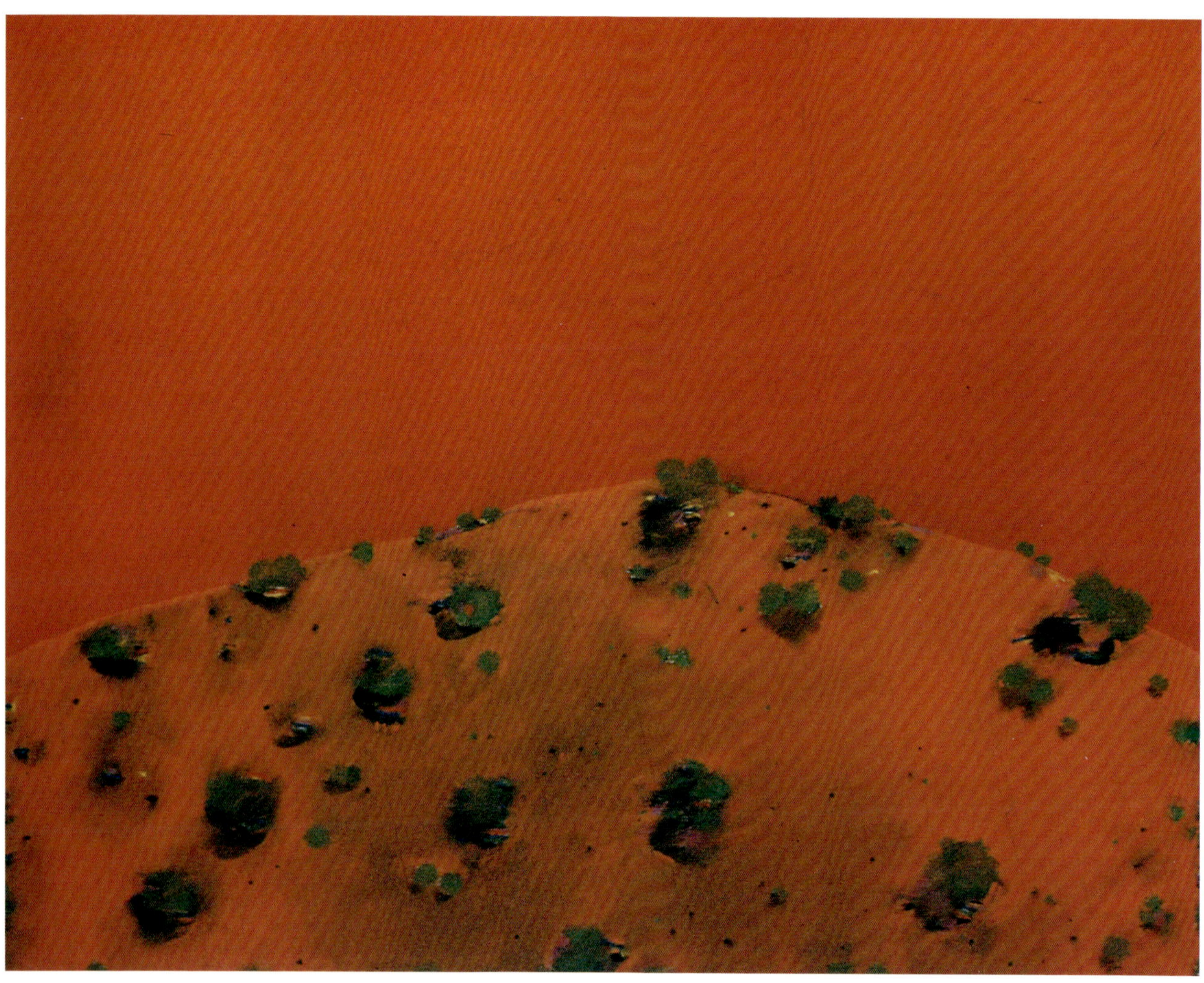

Sand Dune — Central Australia, 1972
Pastel
21" × 25"
Private Collection

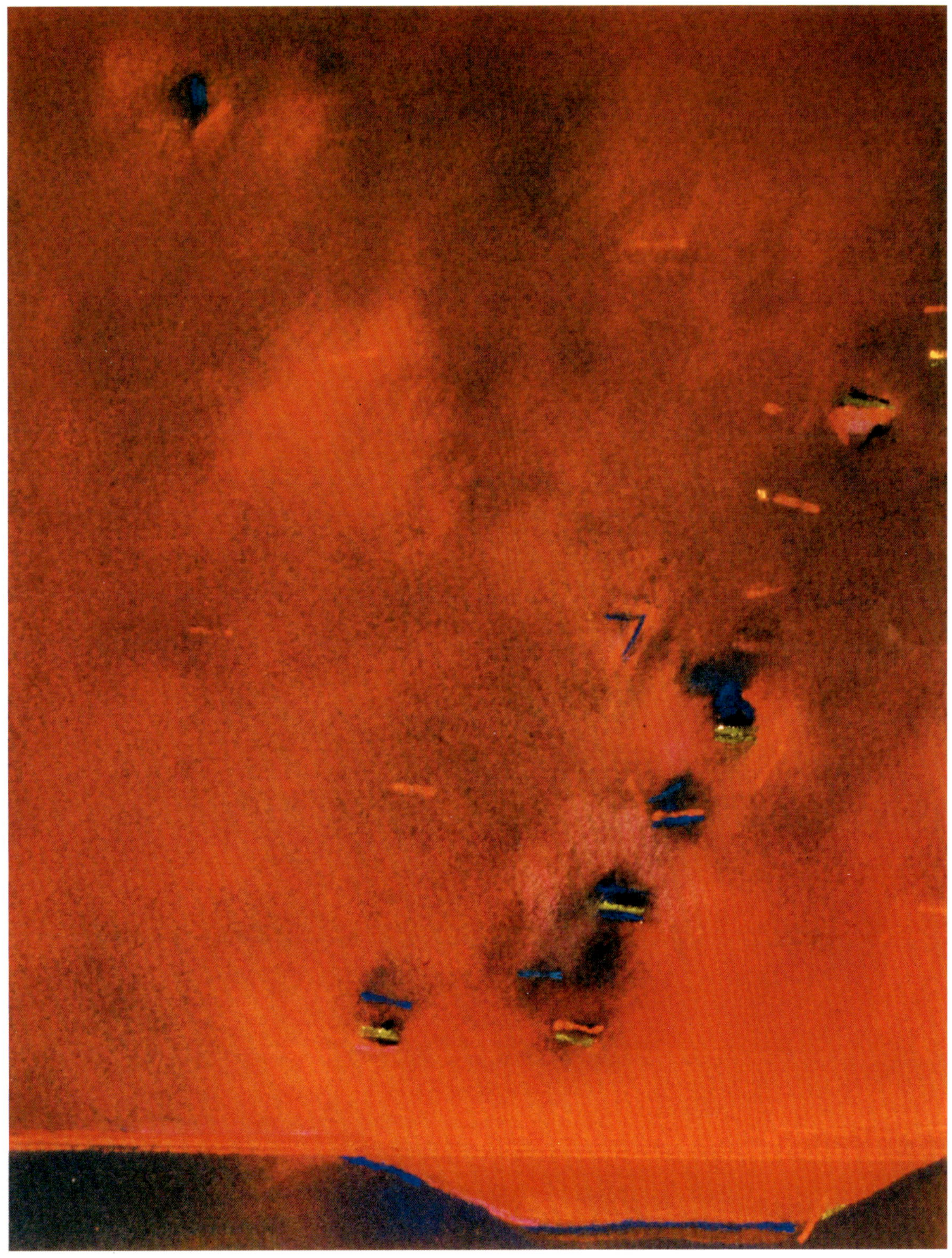

Flight of Birds — Central Australia, 1973
Pastel
$15'' \times 11^{1}/_{2}''$
Private Collection

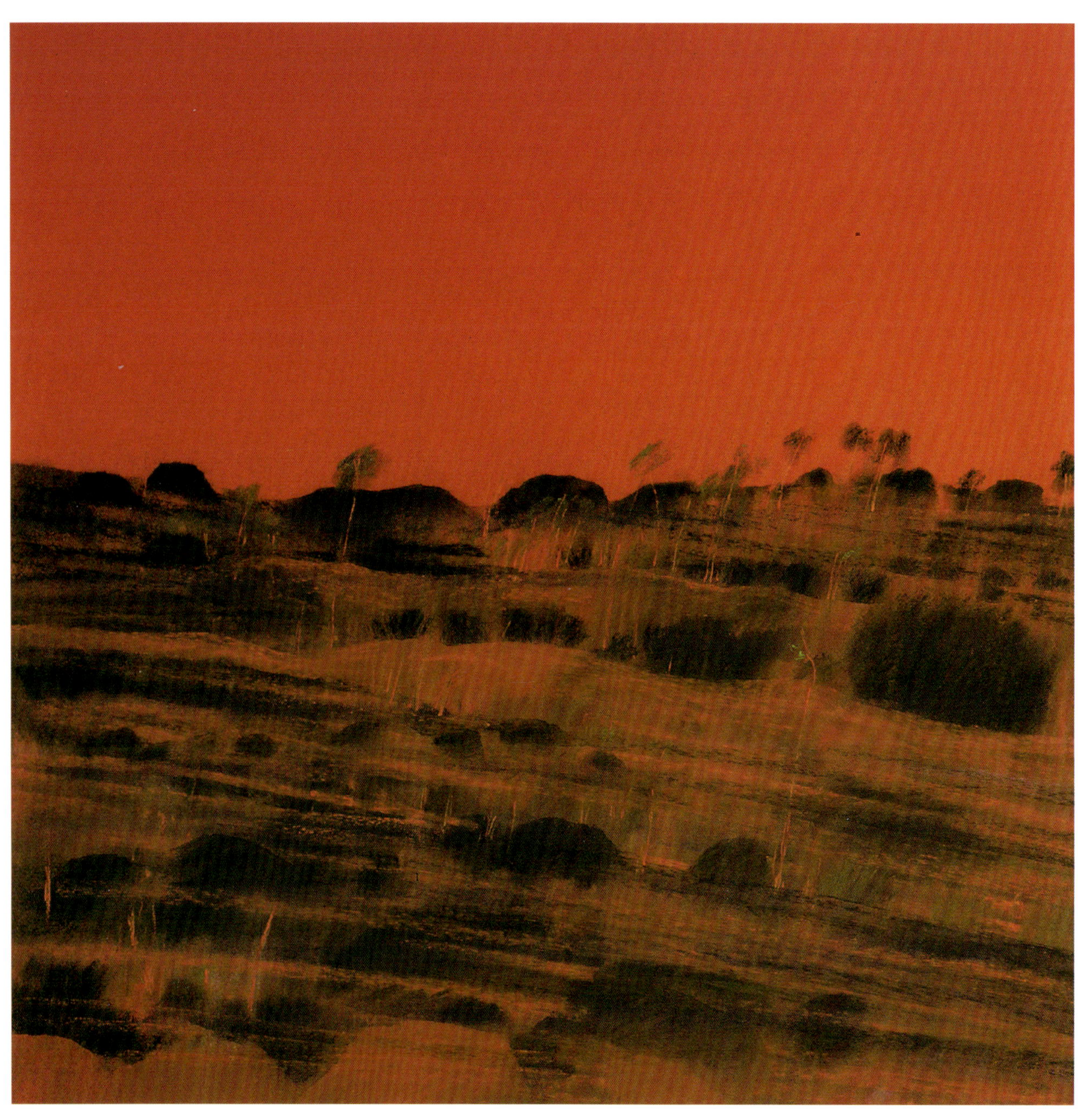

Red Landscape — Central Australia, 1973
Pastel
25" × 21"
Collection: Ormond College — University of Melbourne

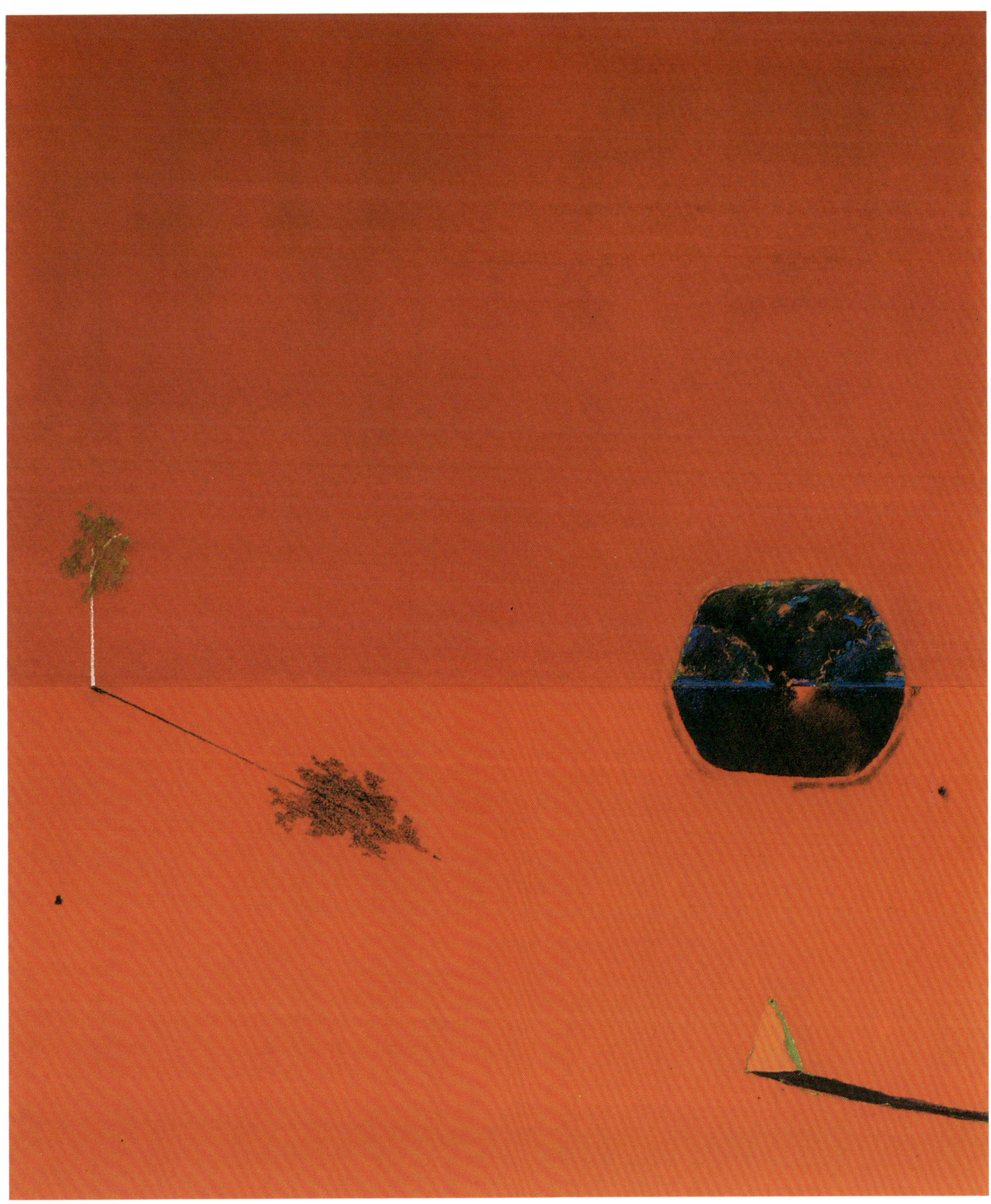

Anthill, Tree & Shadow — Central Australia, 1973
Pastel
25" × 21"
Private Collection

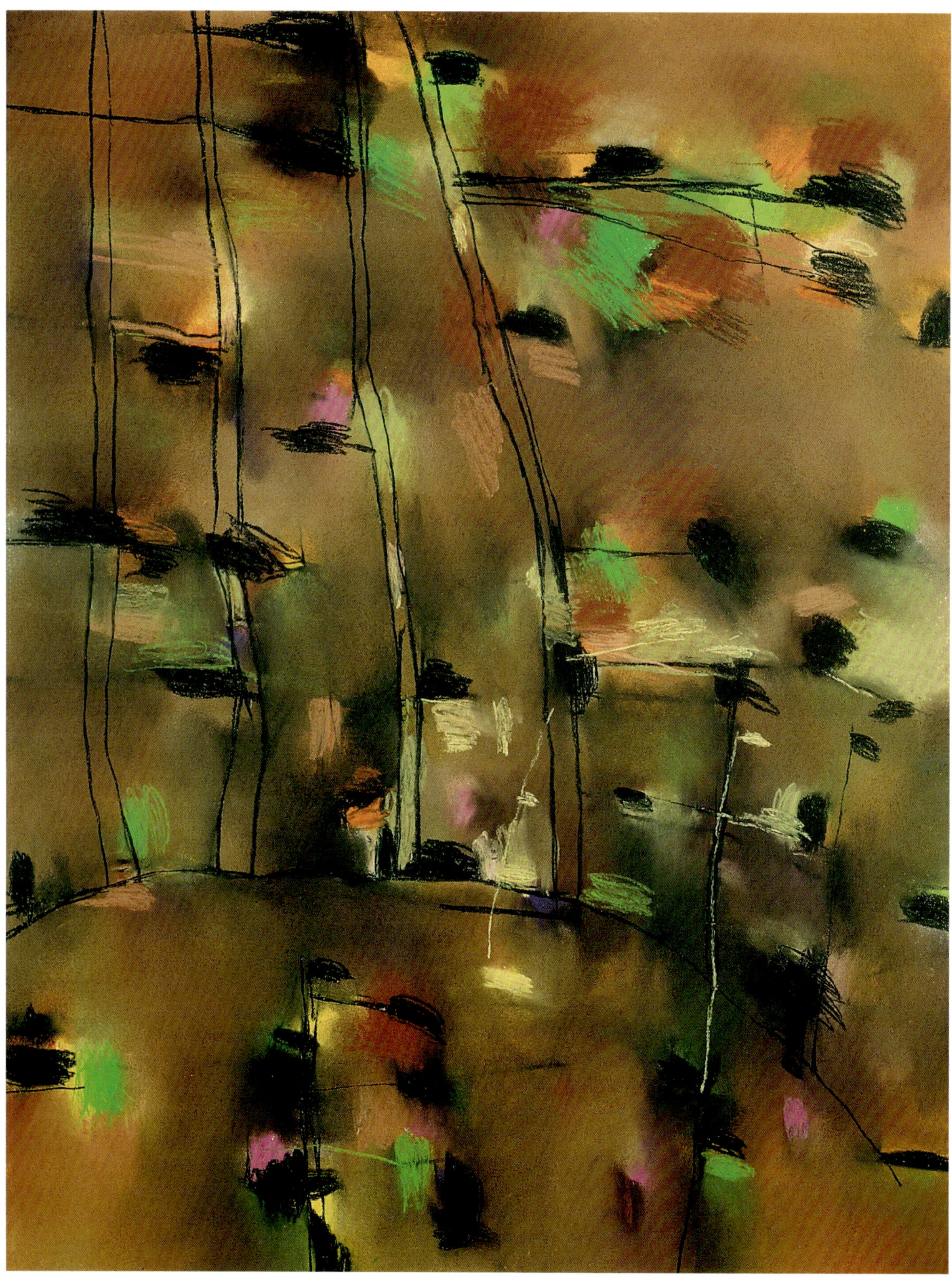

Tree Study, 1982
Pastel
24" × 20 1/2"
Private Collection

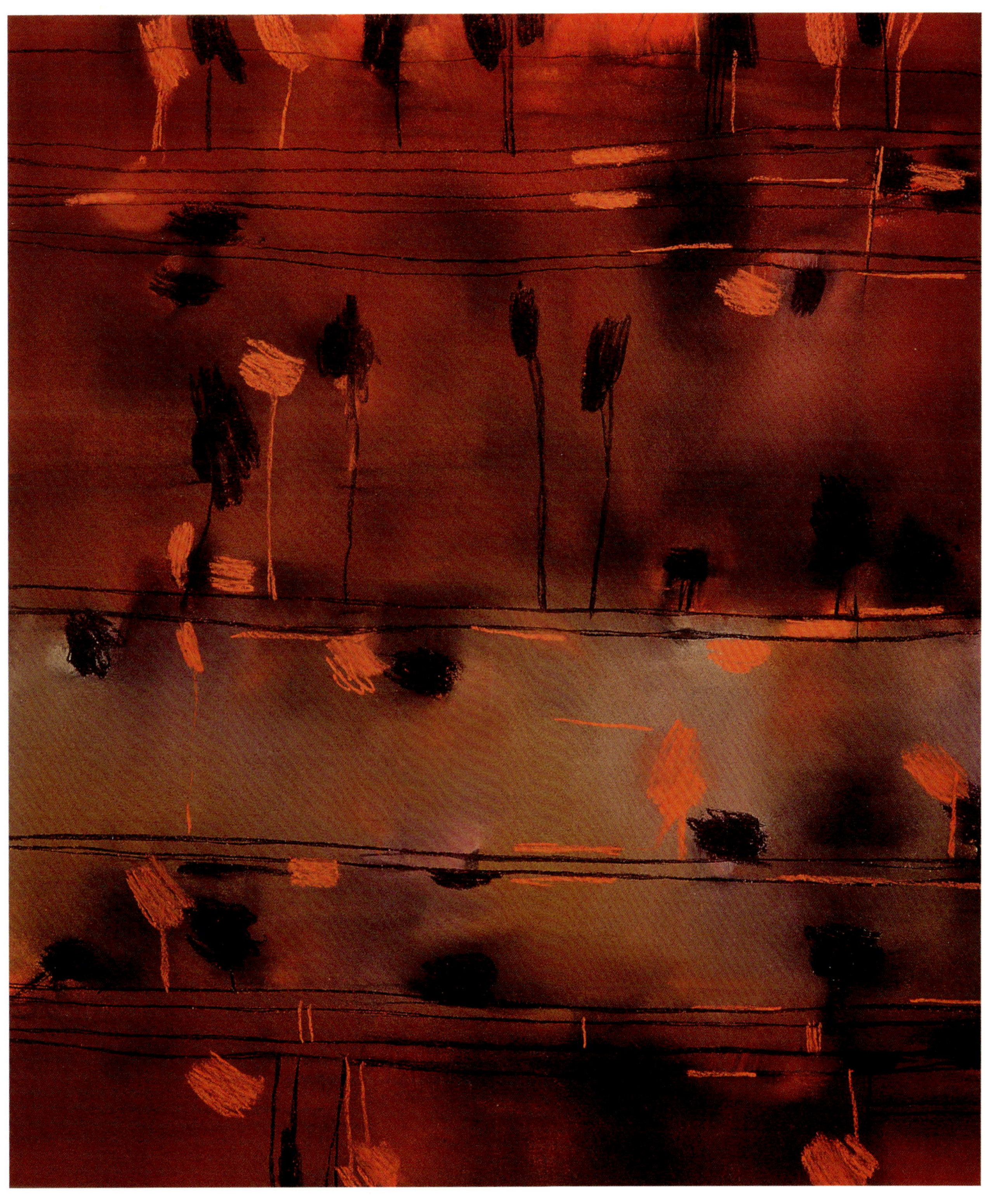

Landscape with Trees & Fields — Northern Australia, 1984
Pastel
23½" × 20"
Private Collection

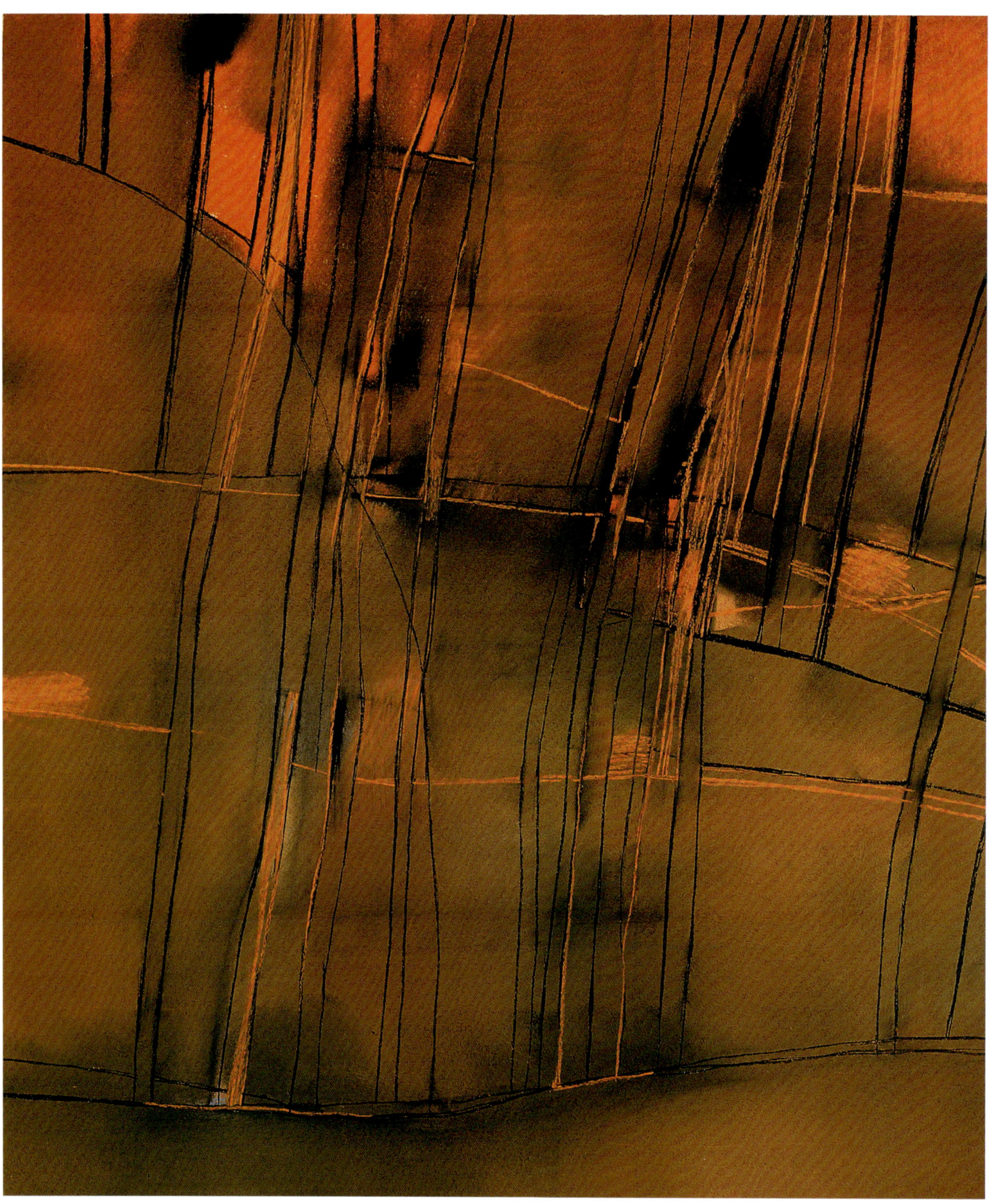

Trees — Central Australia, 1975
Pastel
24" × 20½"
Private Collection

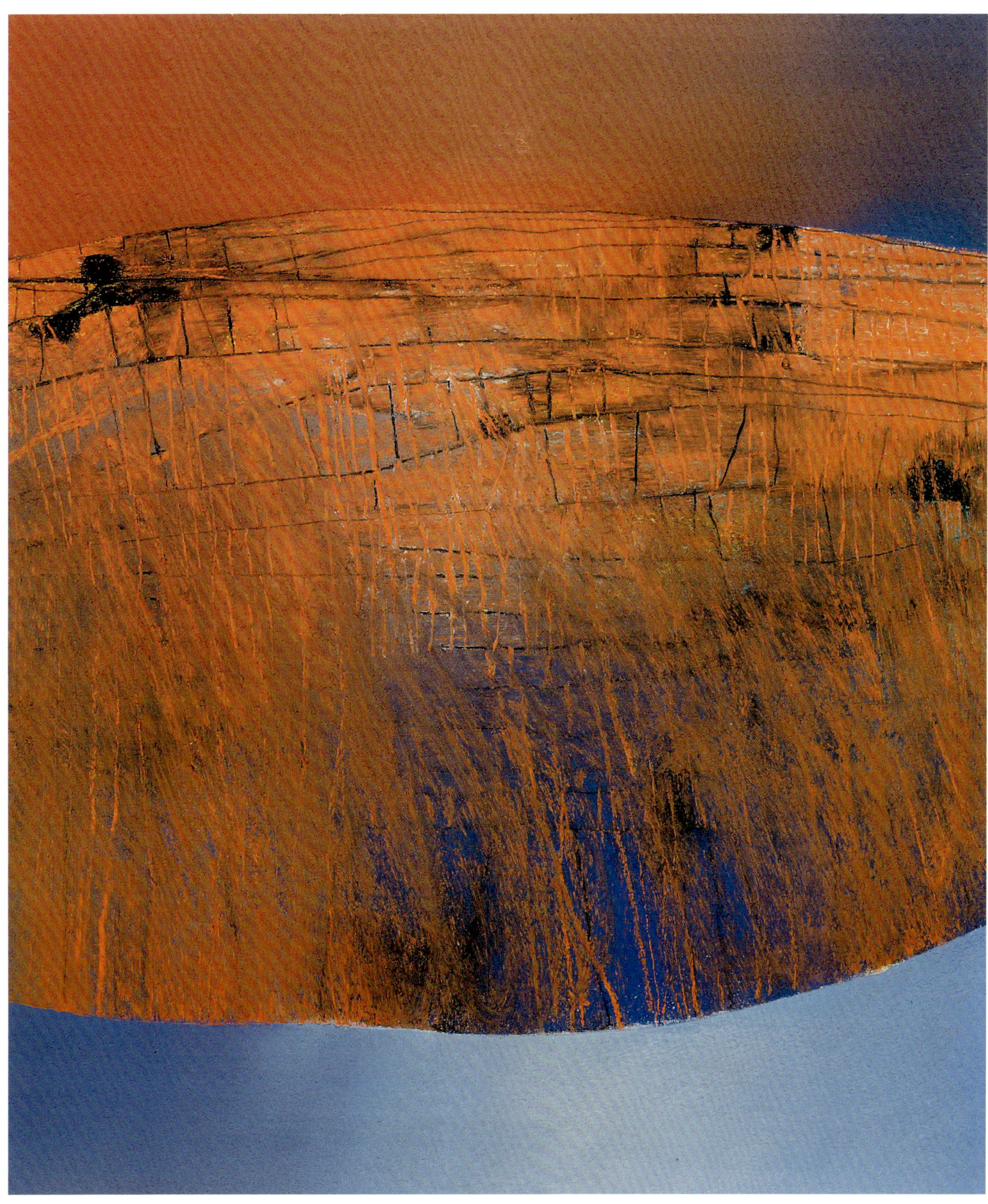

Wooded Landscape — Northern Victoria, 1990
Pastel
16" × 13 1/2"
Private Collection

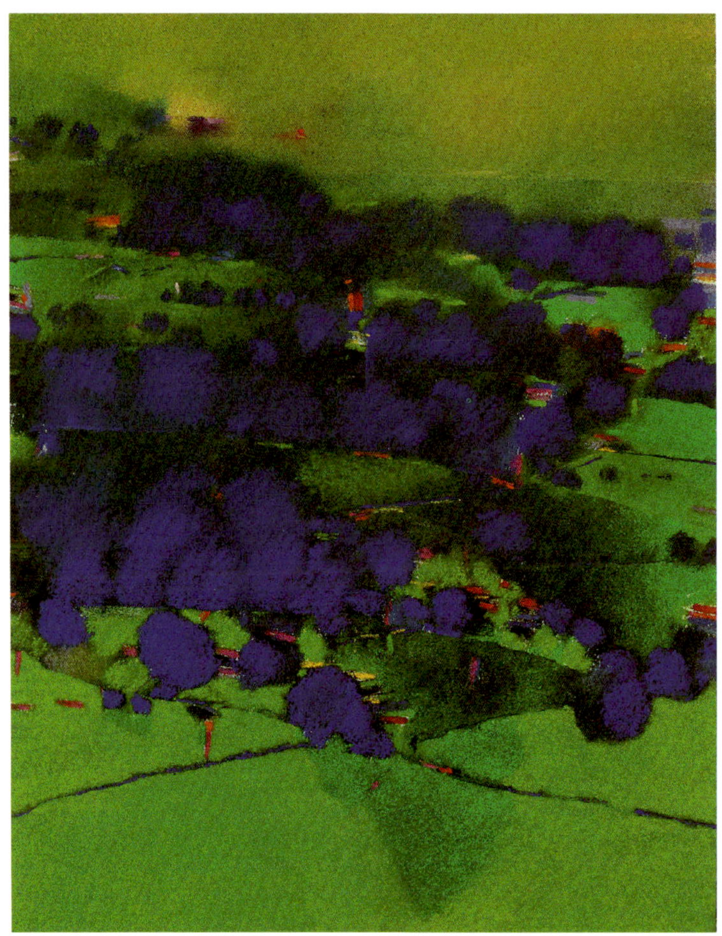

The Creation of Landscape (detail), 1971–75
Pastel
$14^1/_4$" × $11^1/_2$"
Collection: The Artist

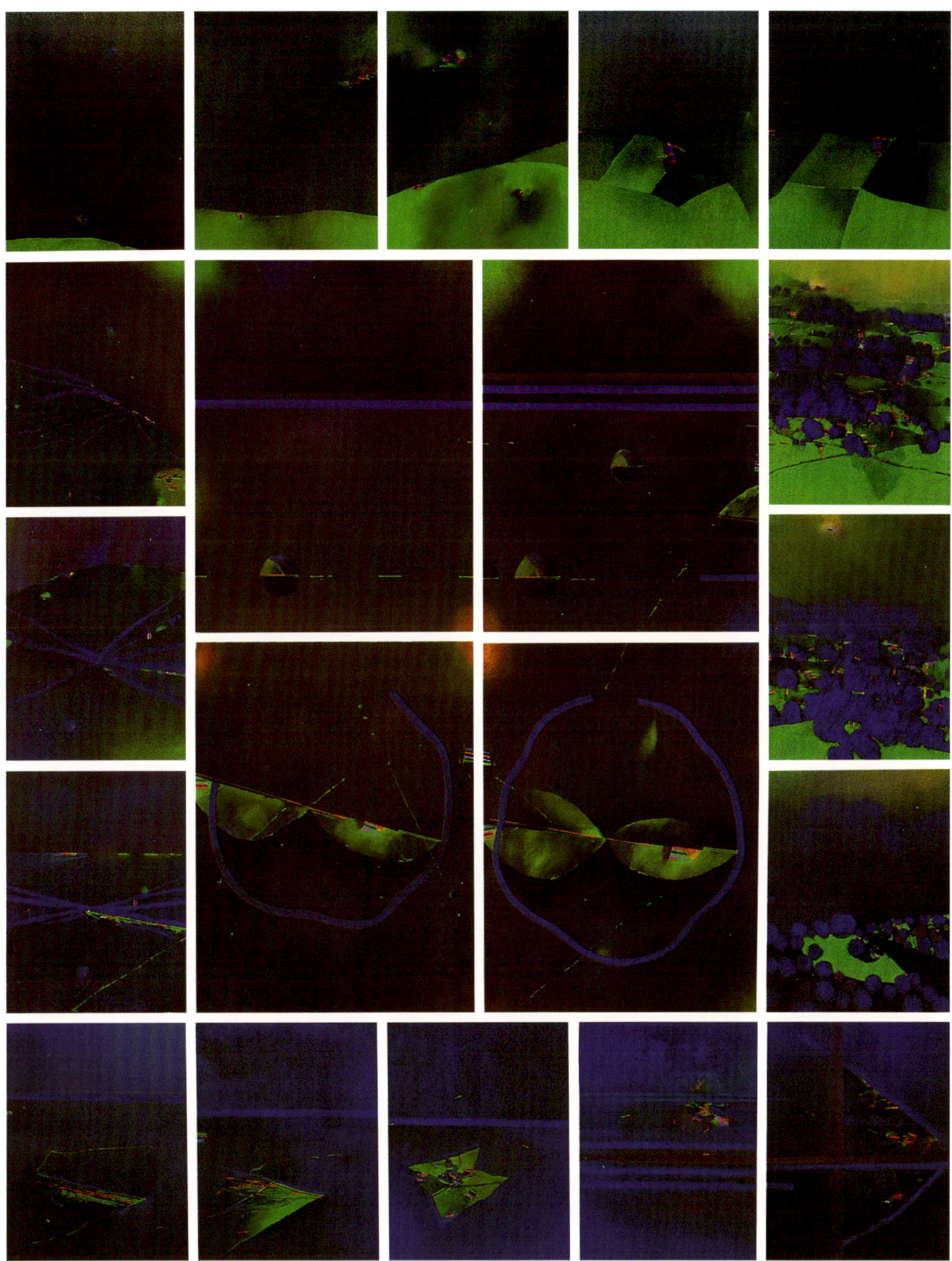

The Creation of Landscape, 1971–75
Pastel
80" × 60"
(Polyptych, 20 pieces)
Collection: The Artist

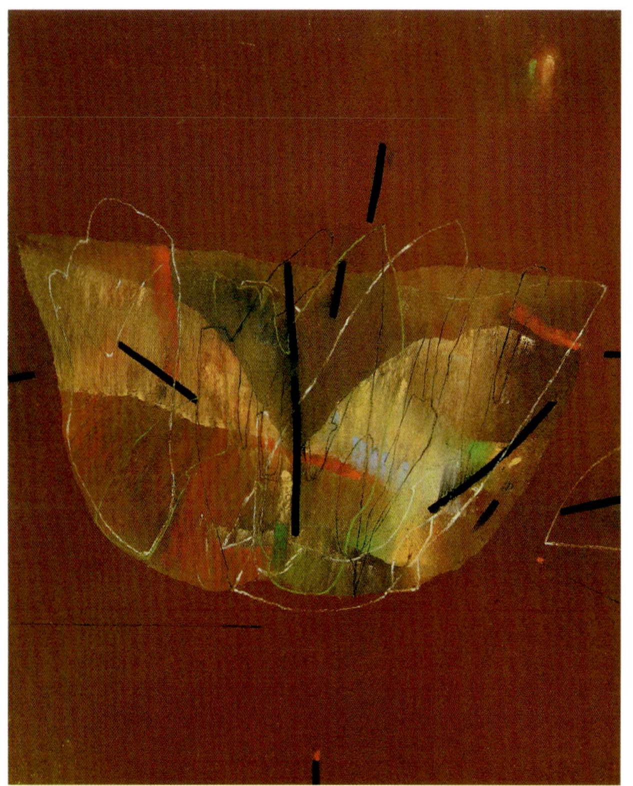

Sixteen Studies on a Ceramic Theme (detail), 1976
Pastel
$14^1/_4$" × $11^1/_2$"
Collection: The Artist

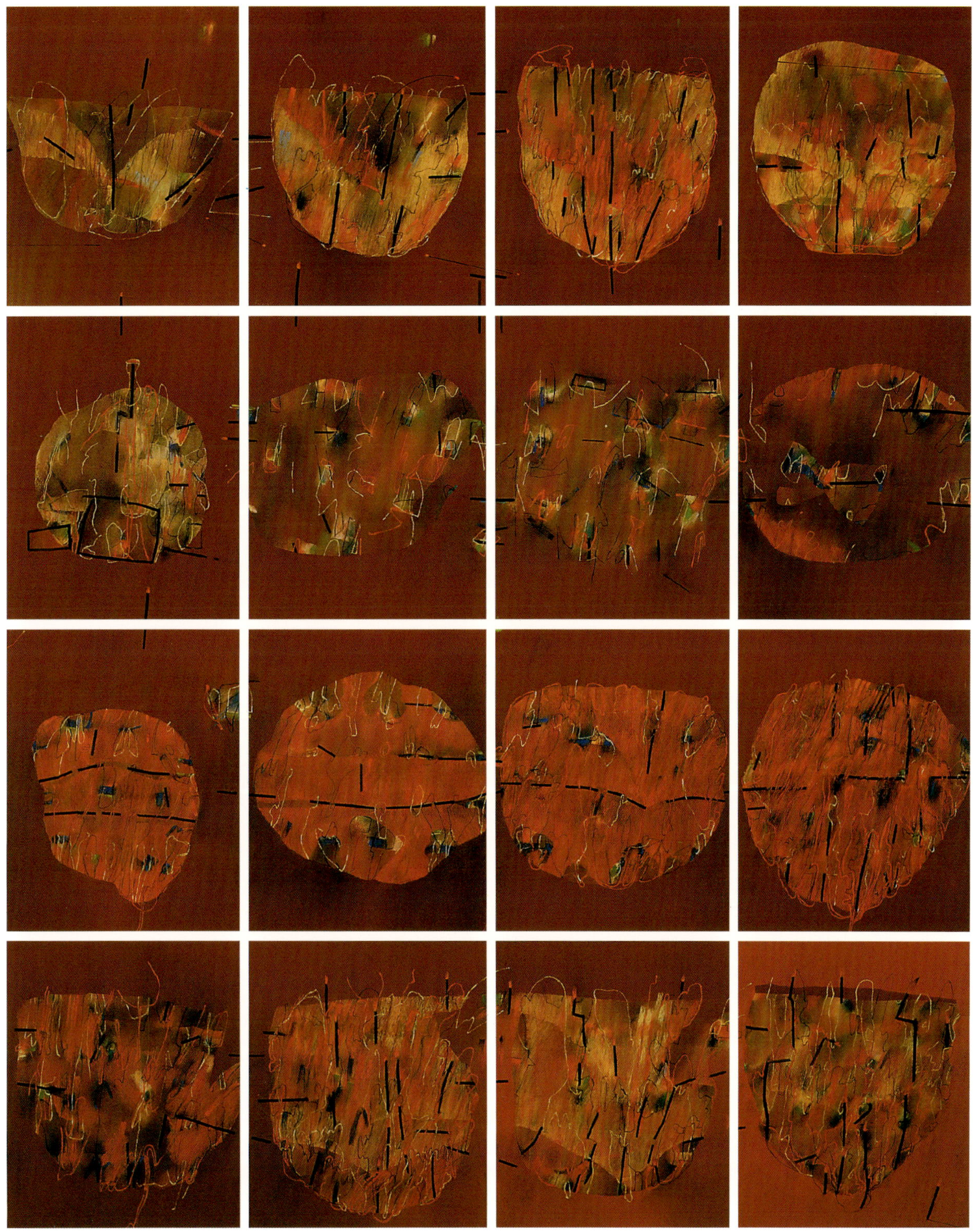

Sixteen Studies on a Ceramic Theme, 1976
Pastel
60" × 65"
(Polyptych, 16 pieces)
Collection: The Artist

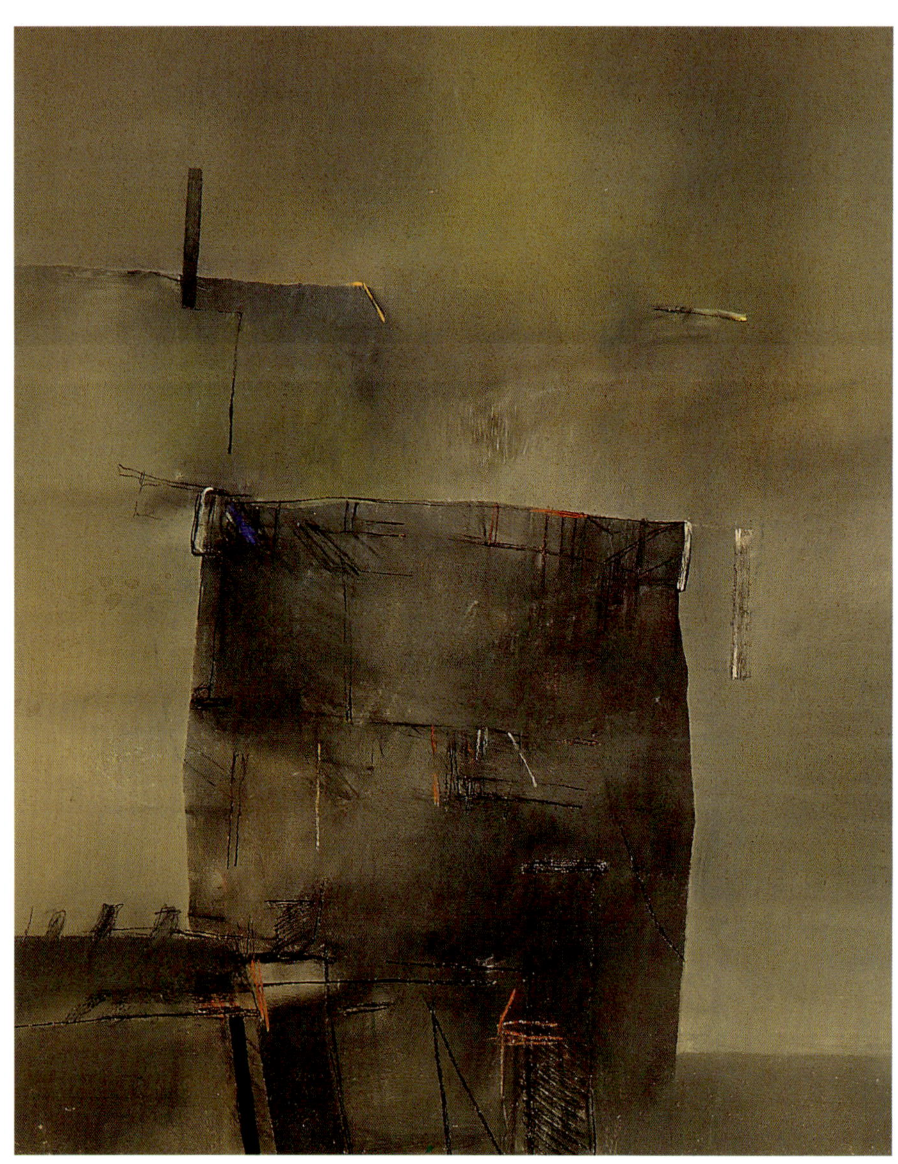

Grey Green Morning with Gasometer, 1979
Pastel
25" × 21"
Collection: Huddersfield Art Gallery

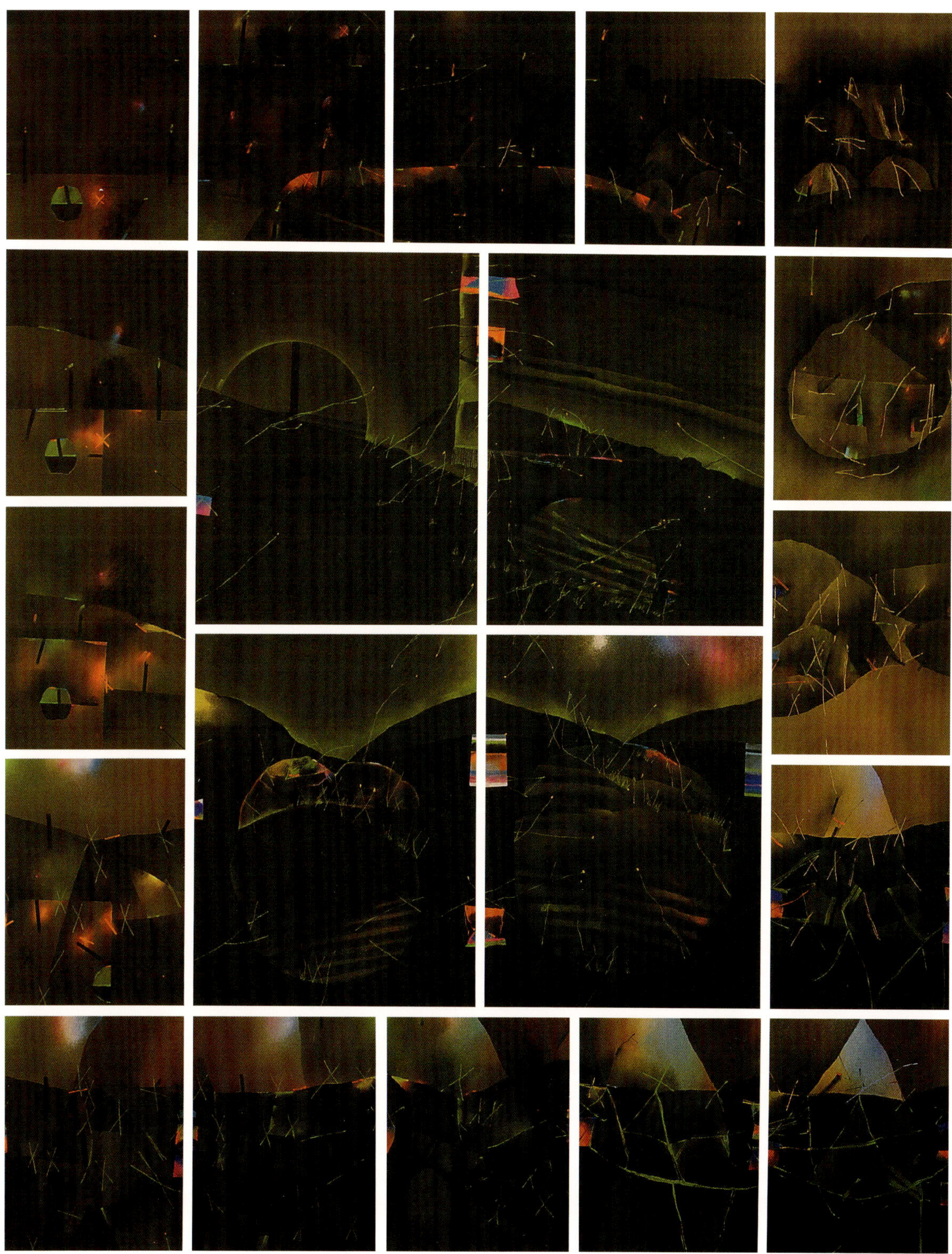

The Creation, 1976
Pastel
80" × 60"
(Polyptych, 20 pieces)
Collection: The Artist

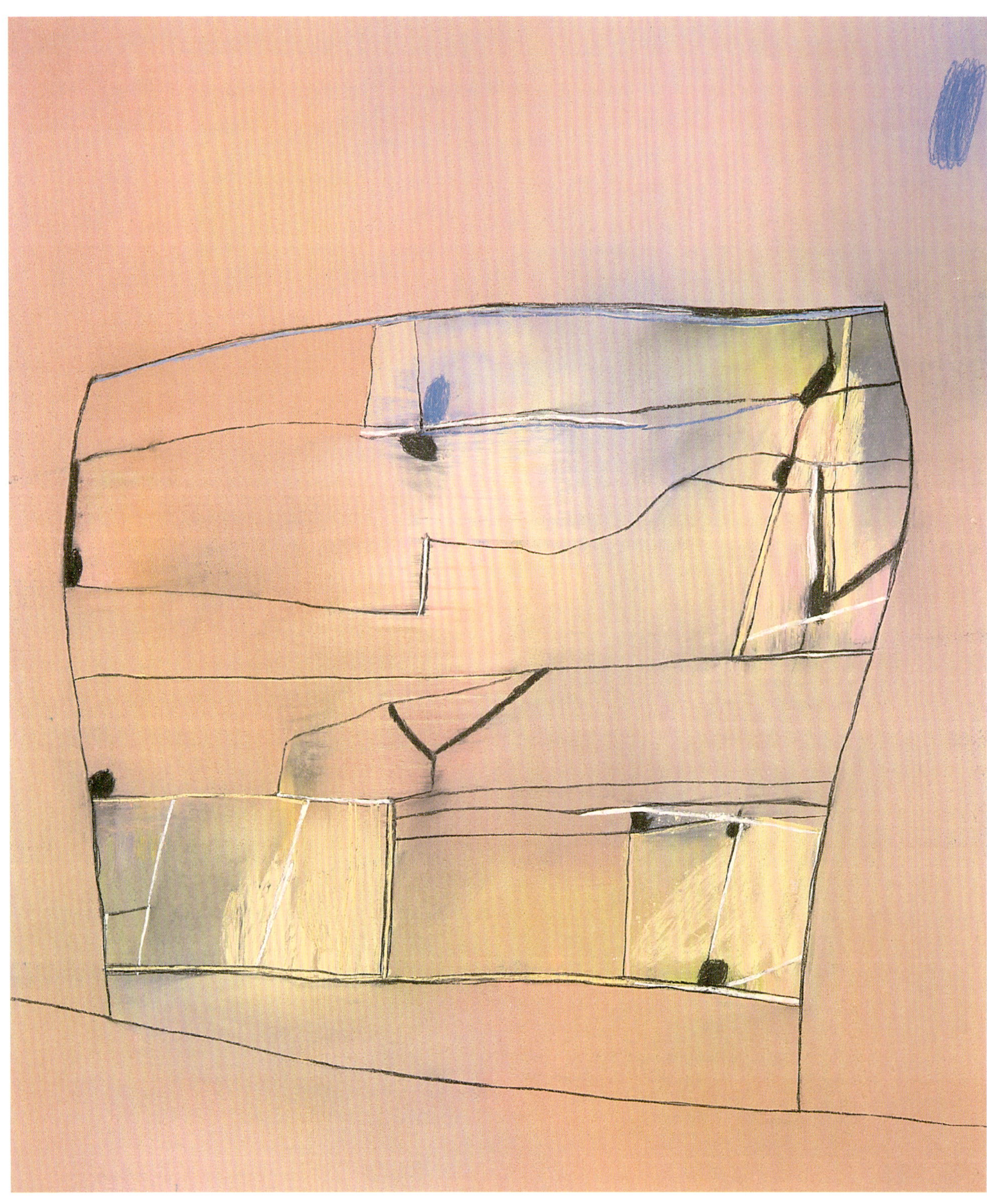

Cliff Landscape, 1985
Pastel
$25^1/_2" \times 21^1/_2"$
Private Collection

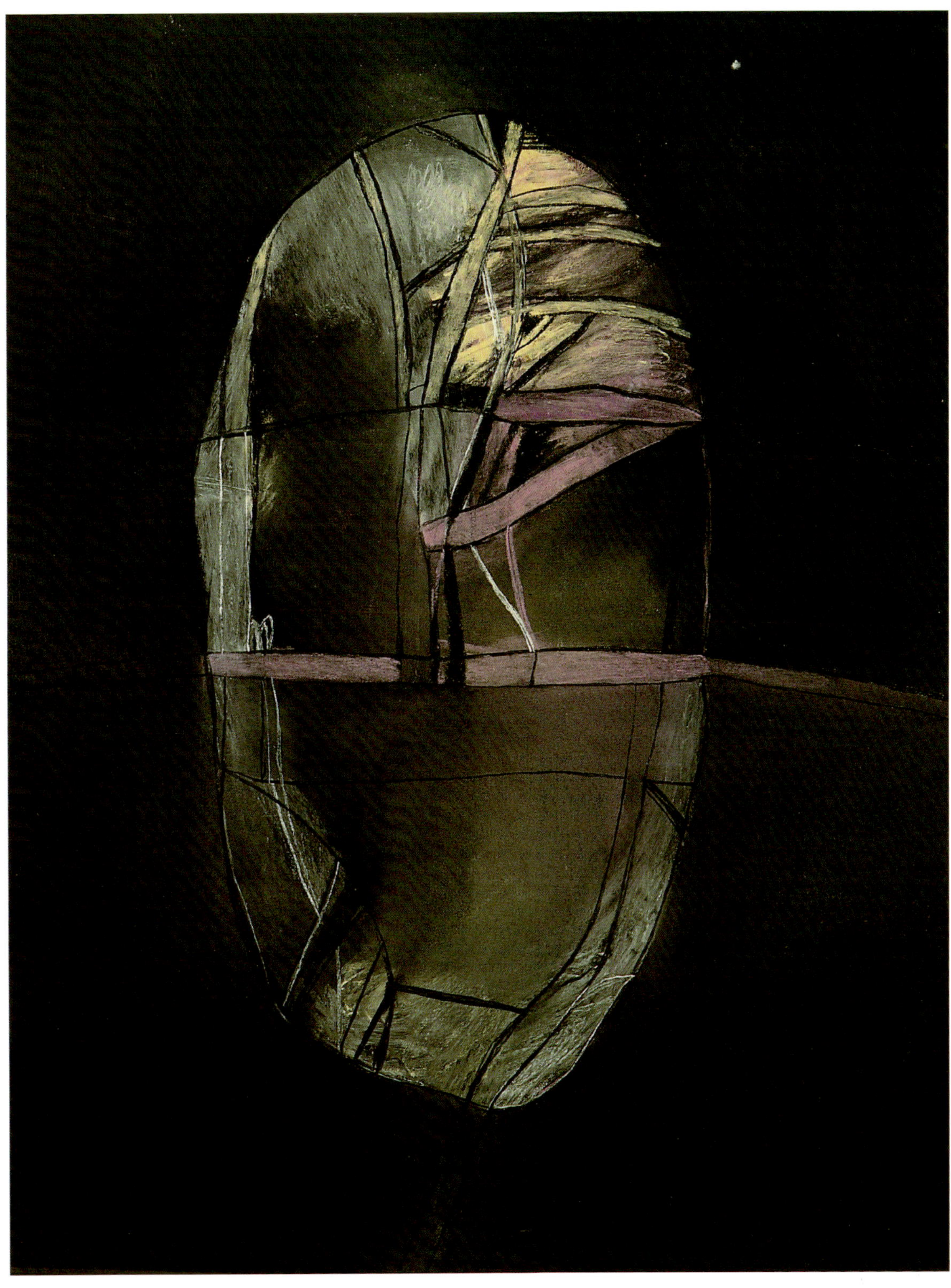

Oval Landscape, 1985
Pastel
$25^{1}/_{2}" \times 20"$
Private Collection

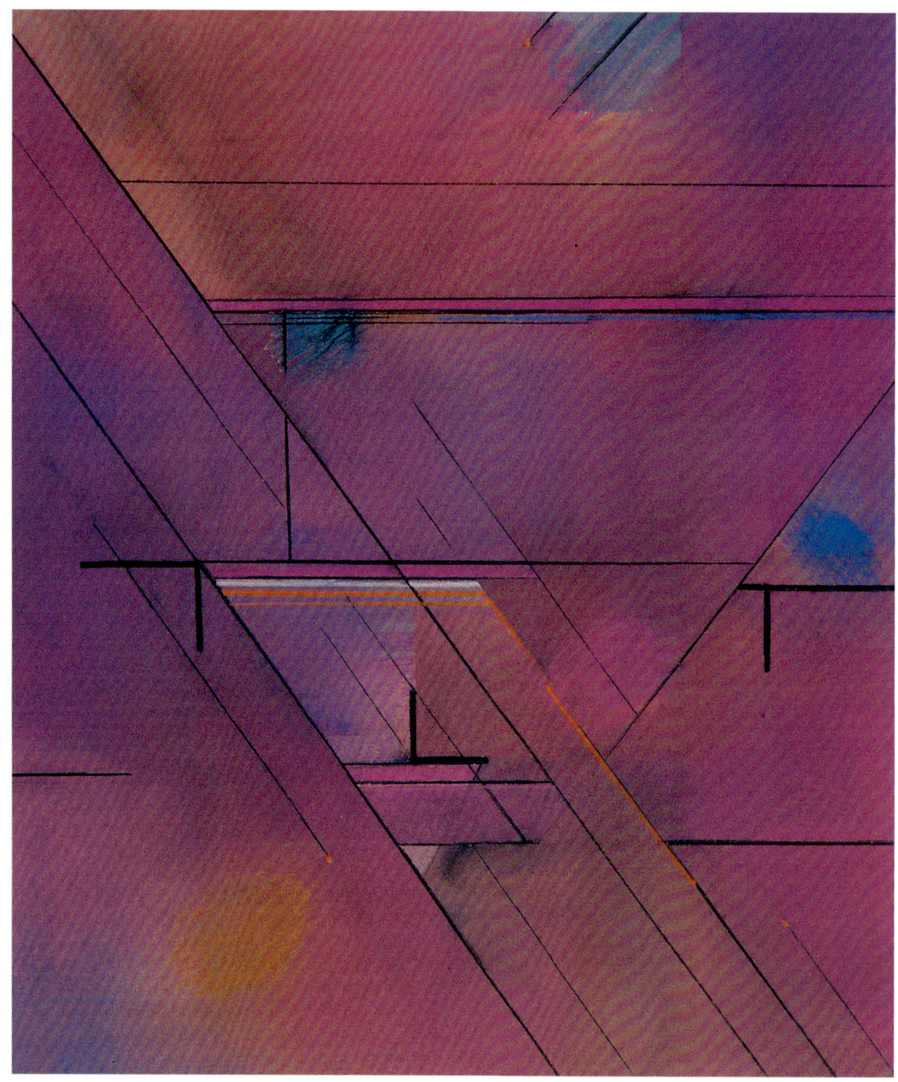

Aerial Freeway, 1984
Pastel
$23^{1}/_{2}" \times 20^{1}/_{2}"$
Private Collection

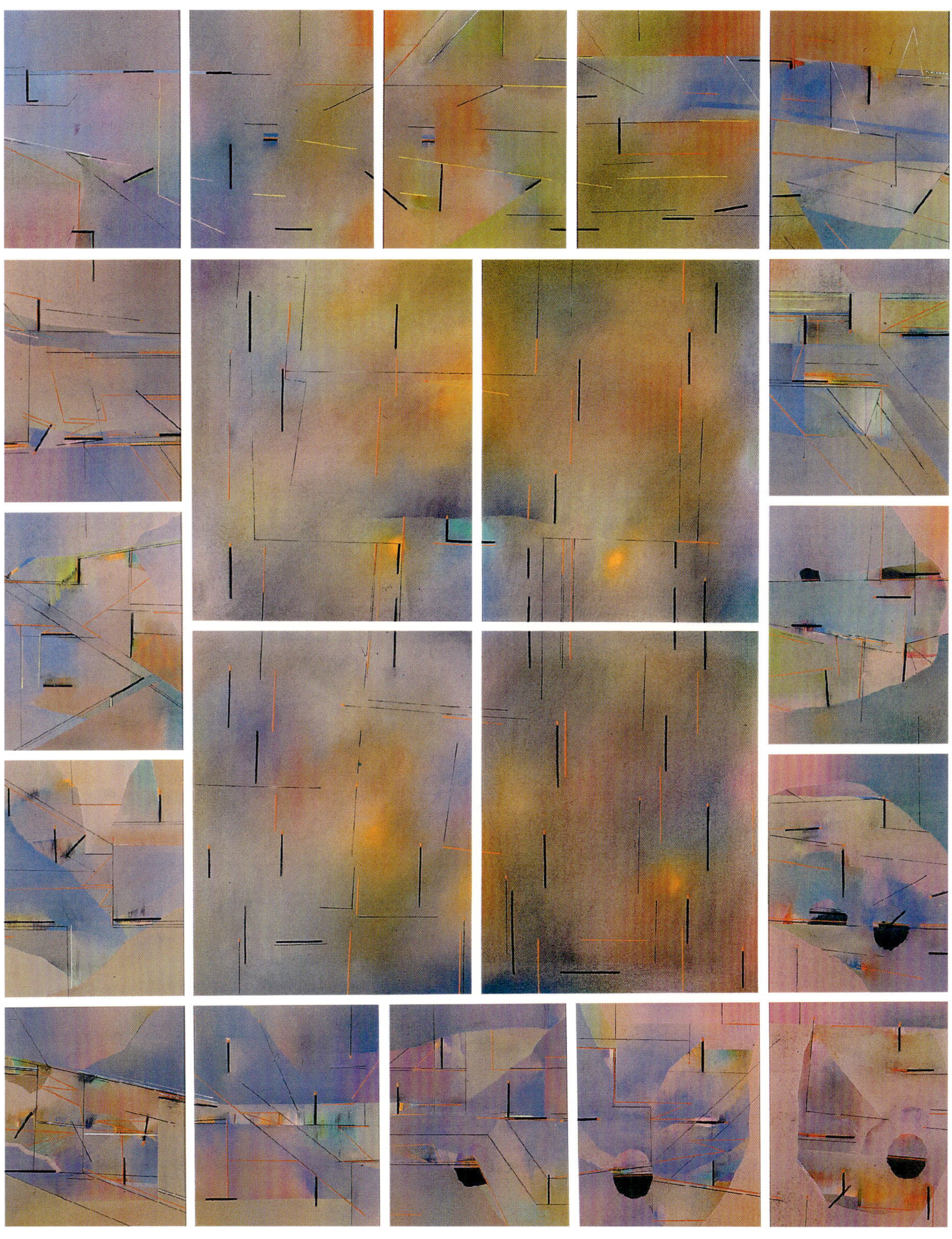

Metropolis I, 1983–86
Pastel
73" × 58 1/2"

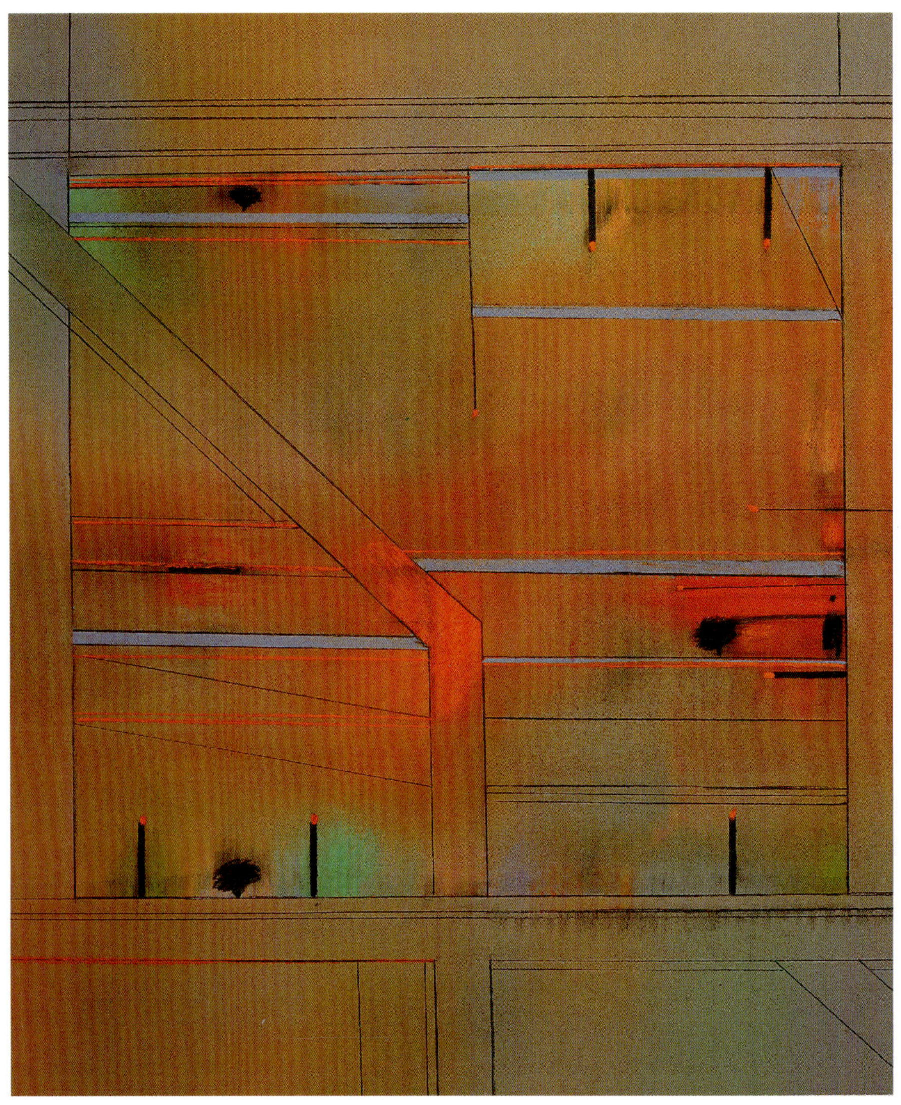

Window — Architectural II, 1986
Pastel
24½" × 21"
Private Collection

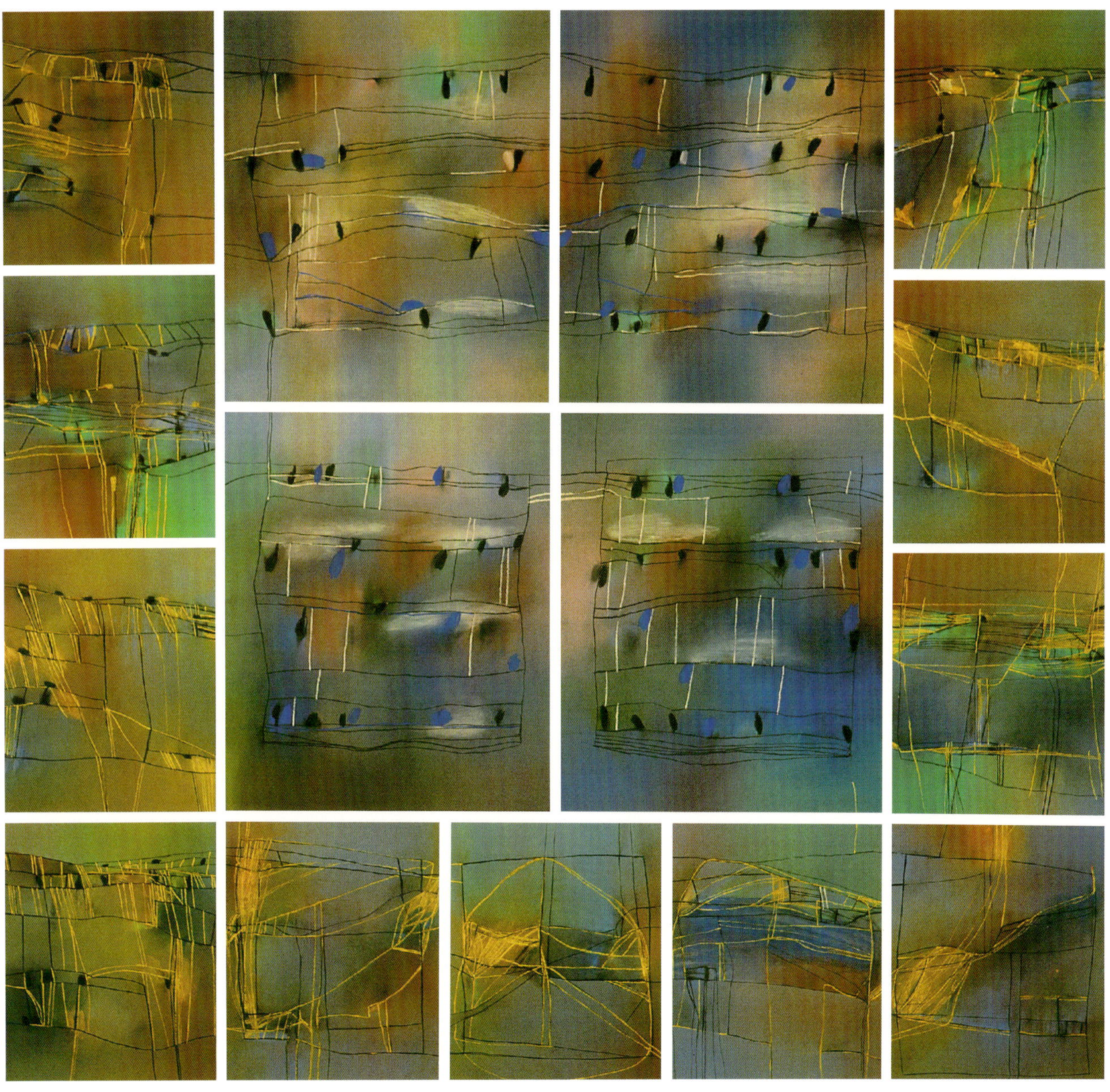

Landscape Vision No. 1, 1986
Pastel
60" × 65"
(Polyptych, 15 pieces)
Private Collection

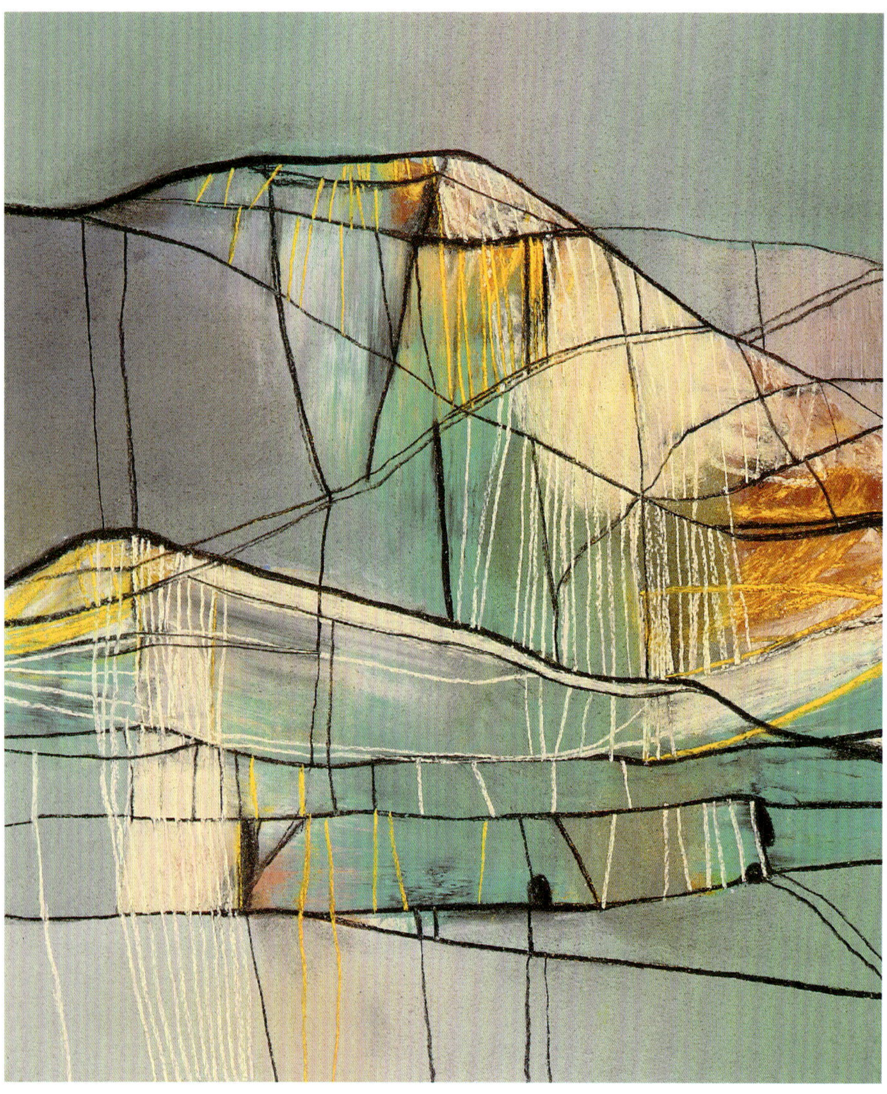

Mountain with Road — Banff, 1987
Pastel
16" × 13 1/2"
Private Collection

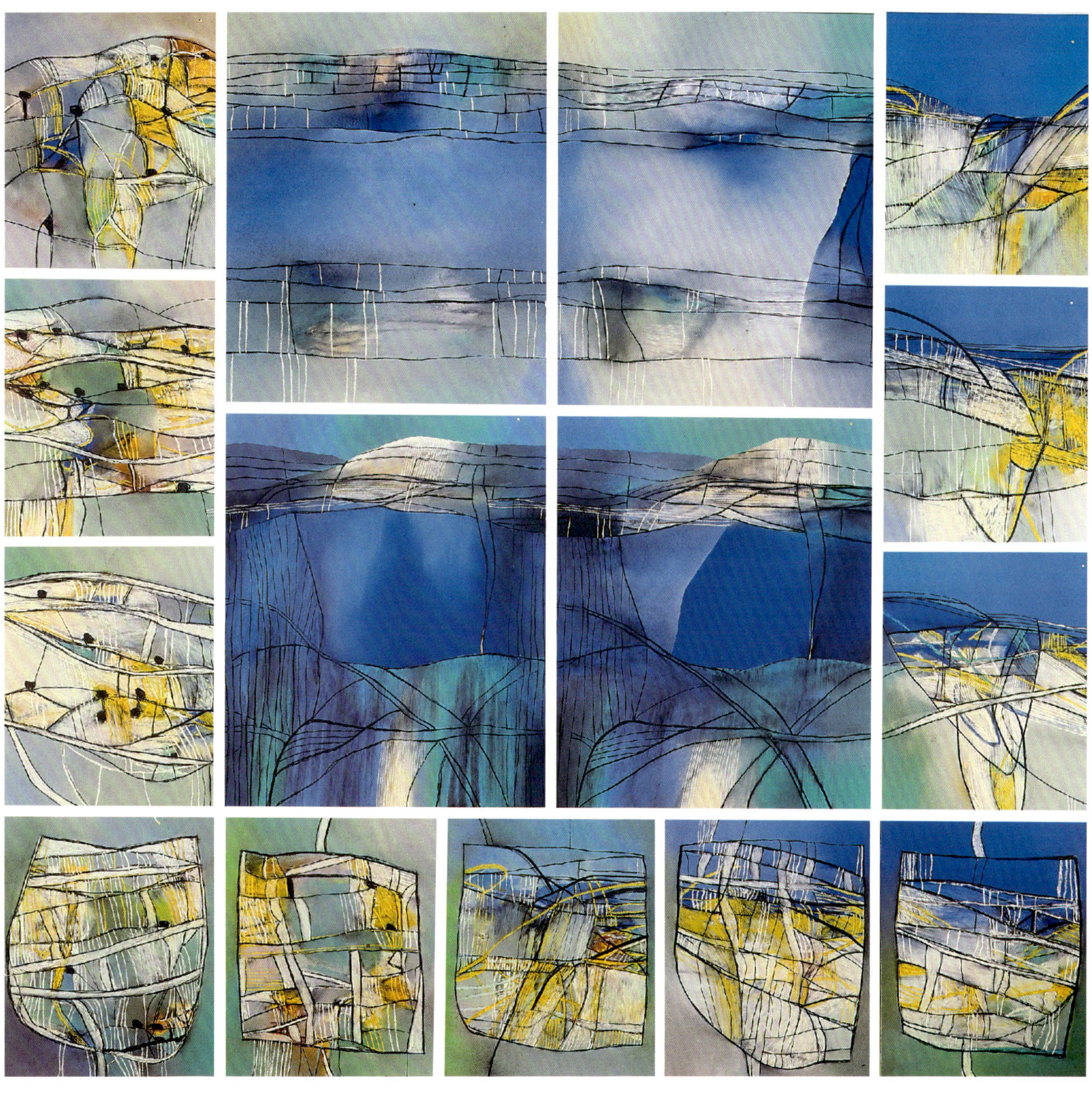

Landscape Vision No. 3, 1988
Pastel
60" × 65"
Private Collection

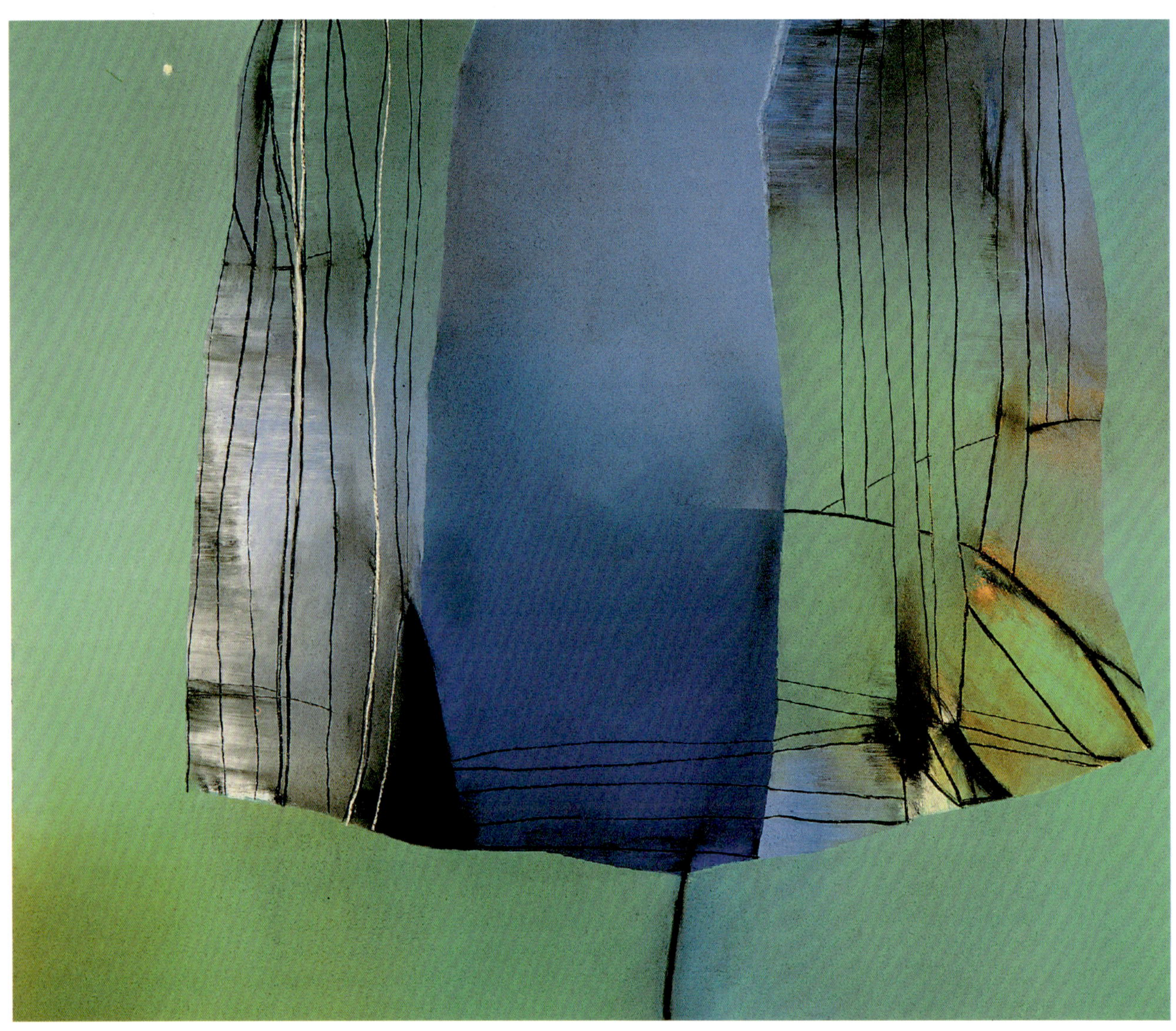

A Mystical View of the Sea, 1988
Pastel
21" × 25½"
Private Collection

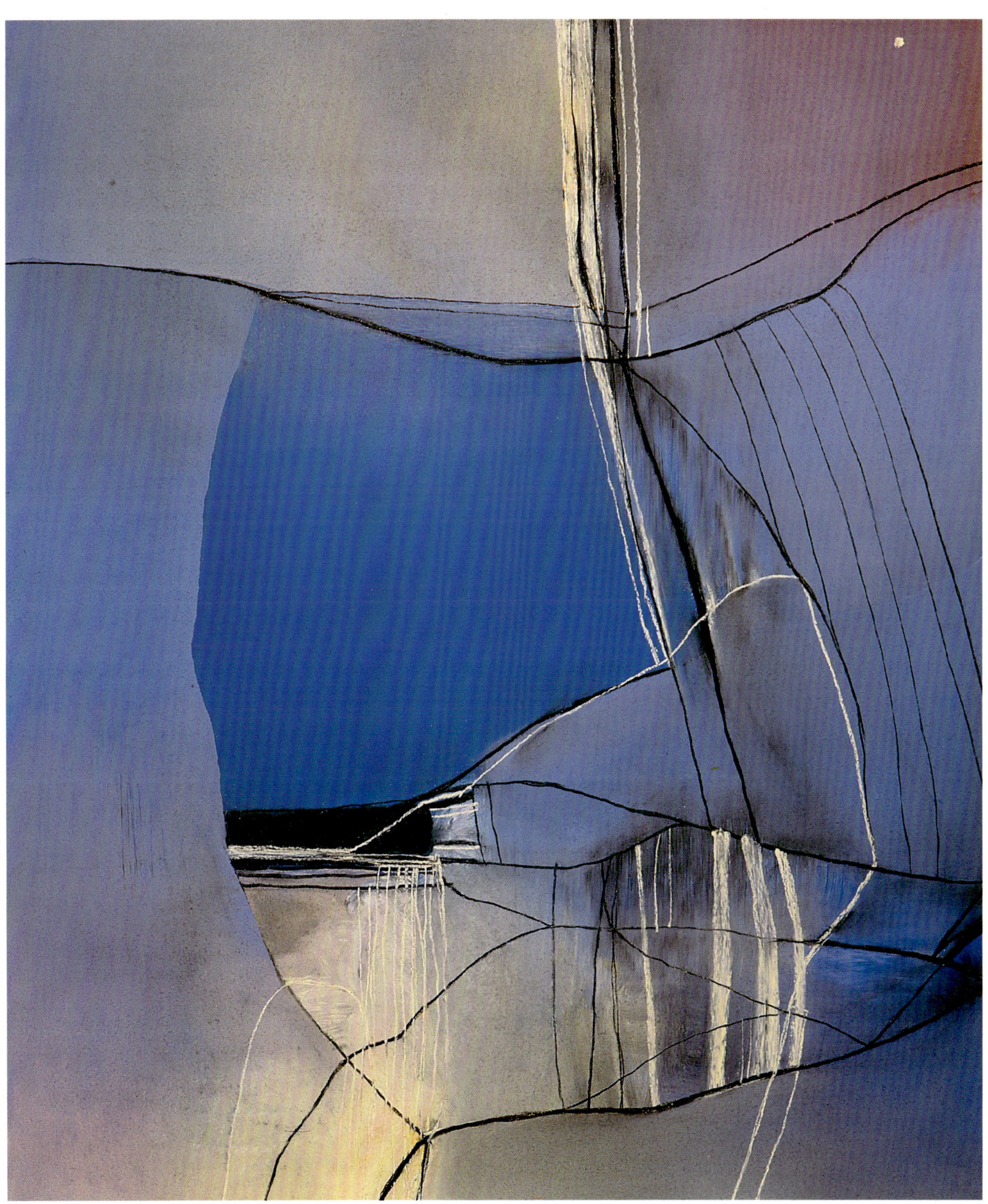

Lake Landscape — Alberta, 1987
Pastel
$25^1/_2$" × 21"
Collection: Yale Center for British Art

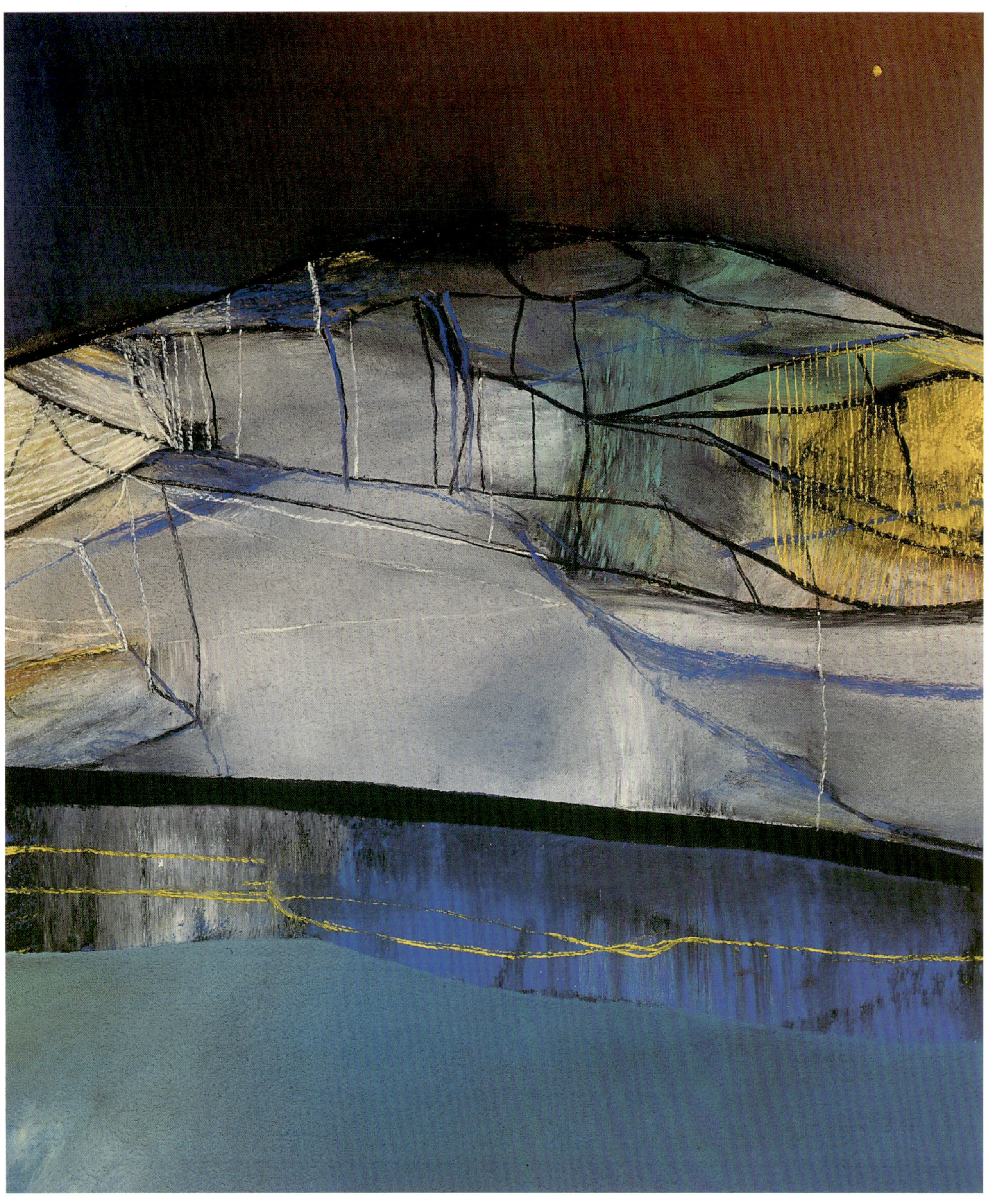

Blue Moorland II, 1989
Pastel
$14^{1}/_{4}" \times 11^{1}/_{2}"$
Private Collection

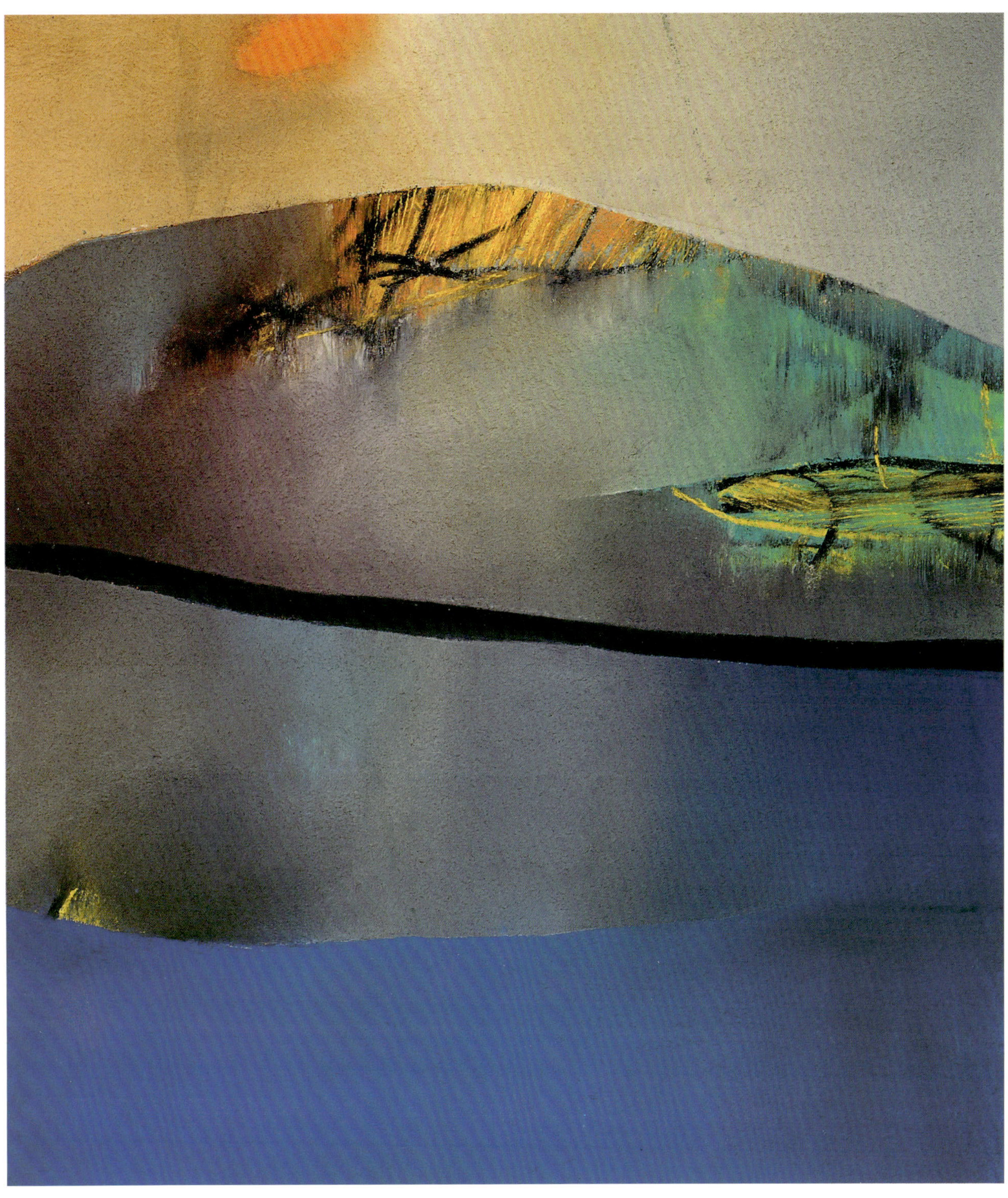

Sunlit Moorland with Wall, 1989
Pastel
14 1/4" × 11 1/2"
Private Collection

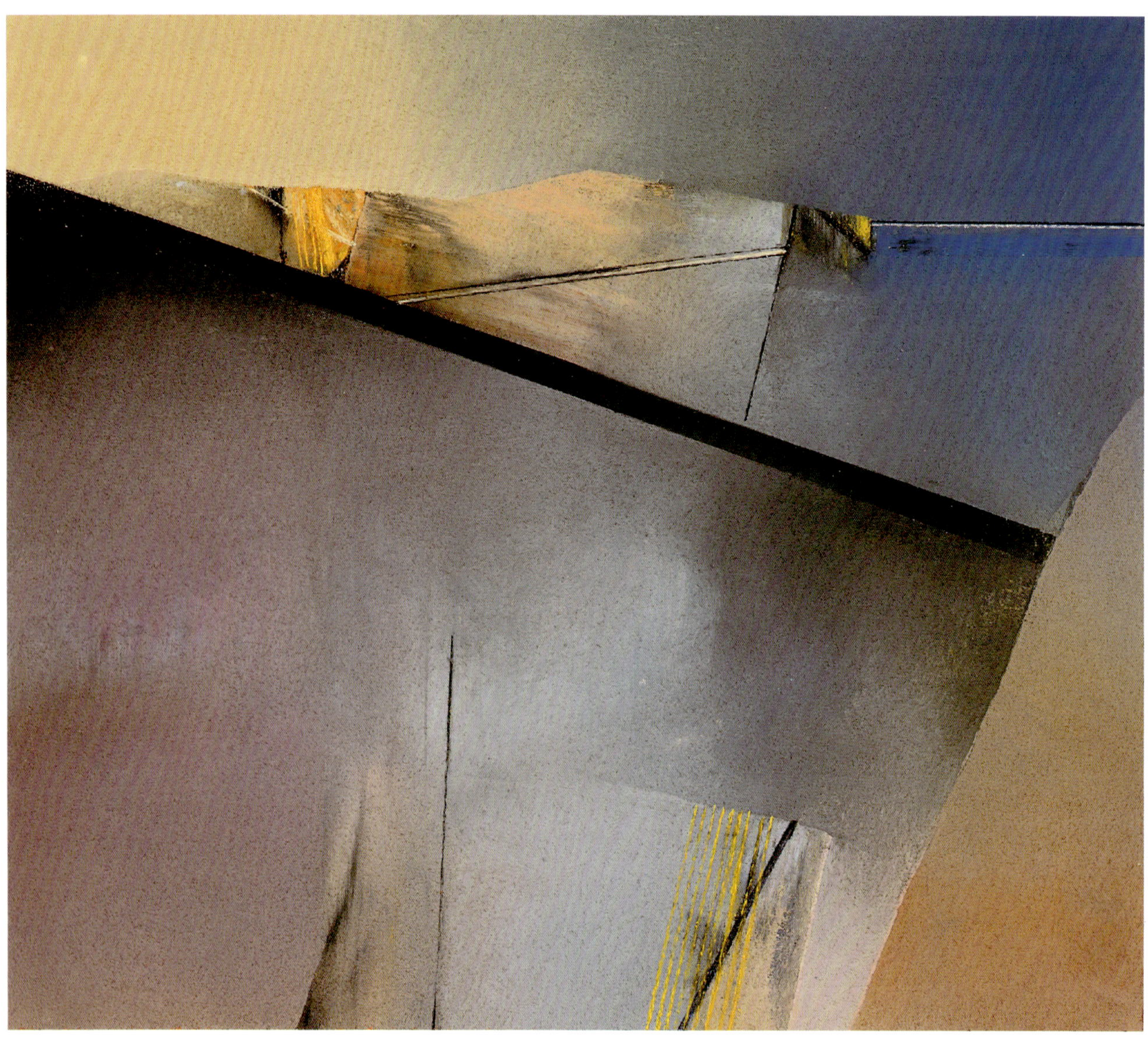

Evening Landscape with Black Wall, 1989
Pastel
14¼" × 17"
Private Collection

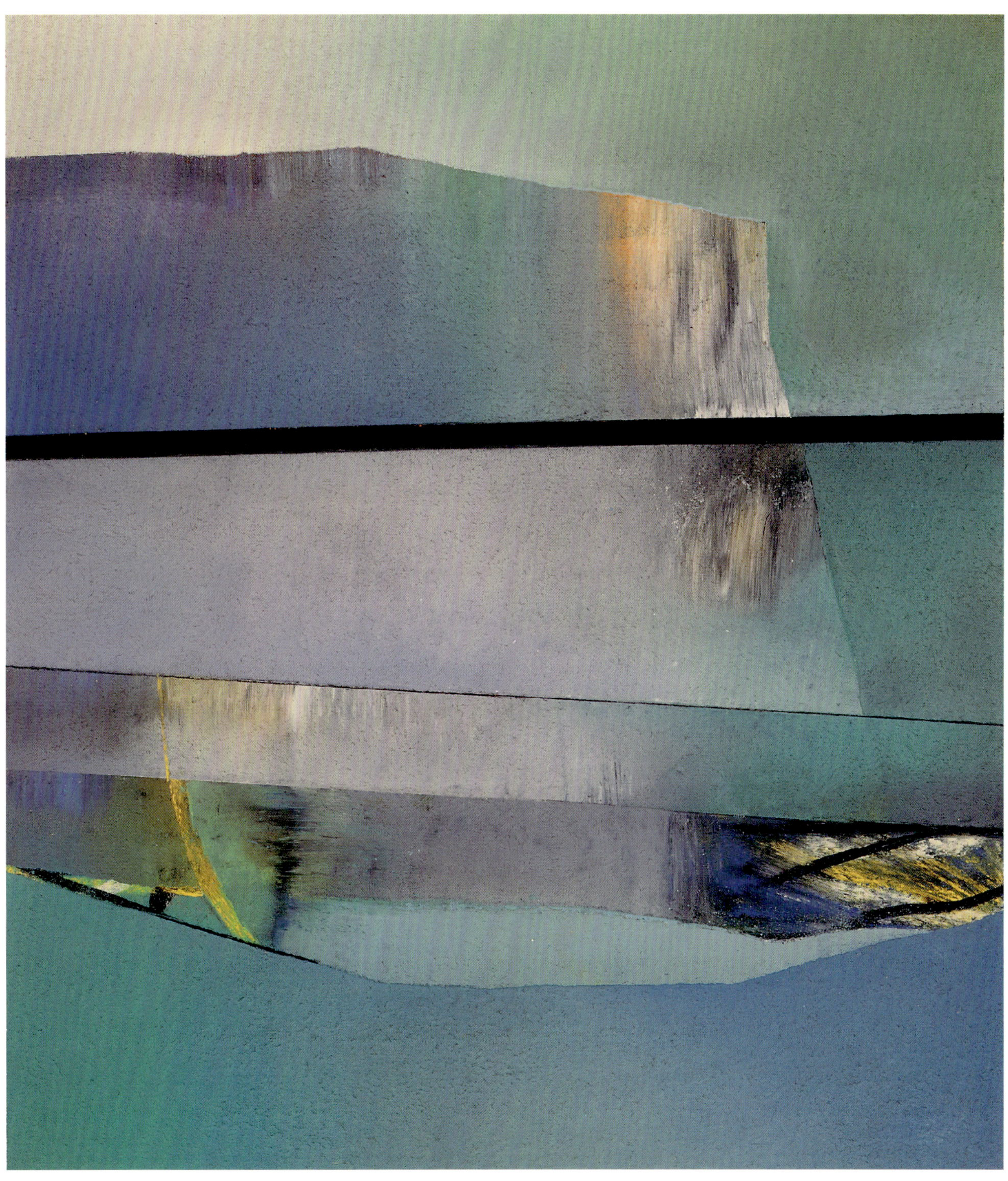

Cliff Seascape, 1989
Pastel
17" × 14 1/4"
Private Collection

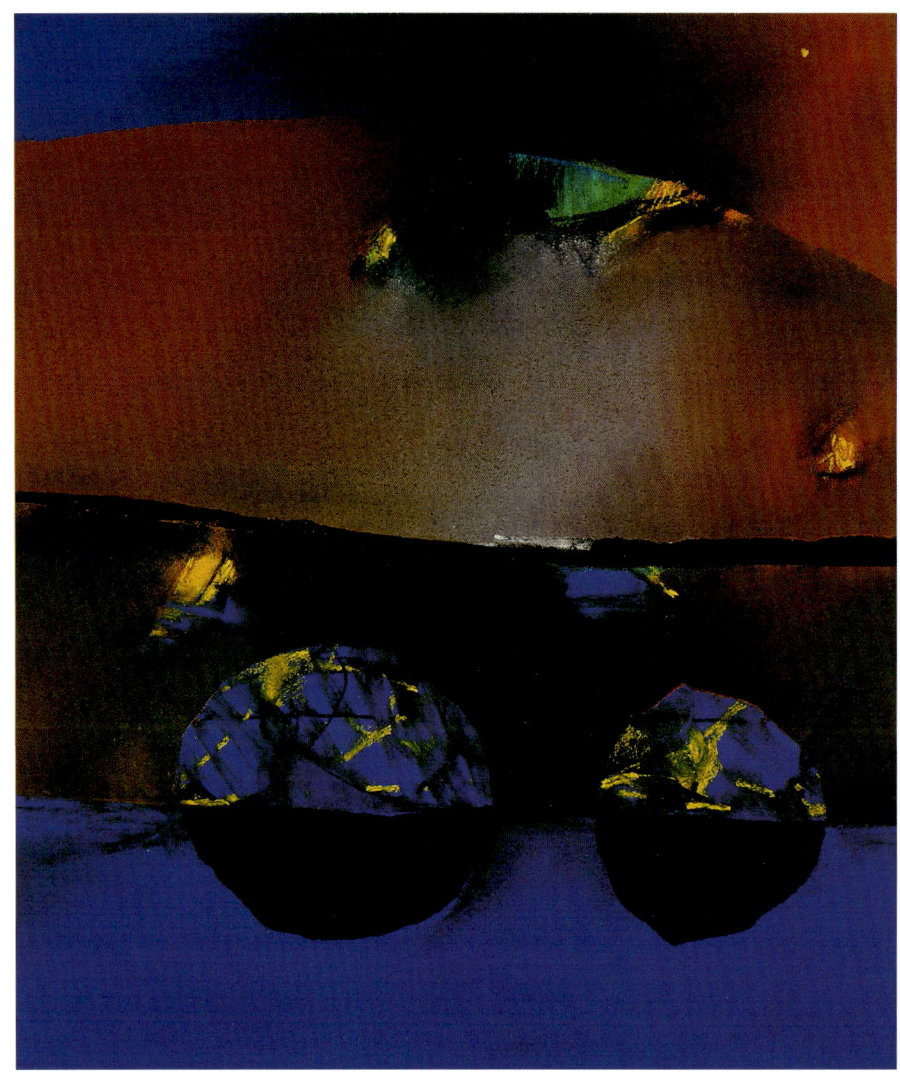

Two Stones and Hillside — Evening, 1990
Pastel
16" × 13½"
Private Collection

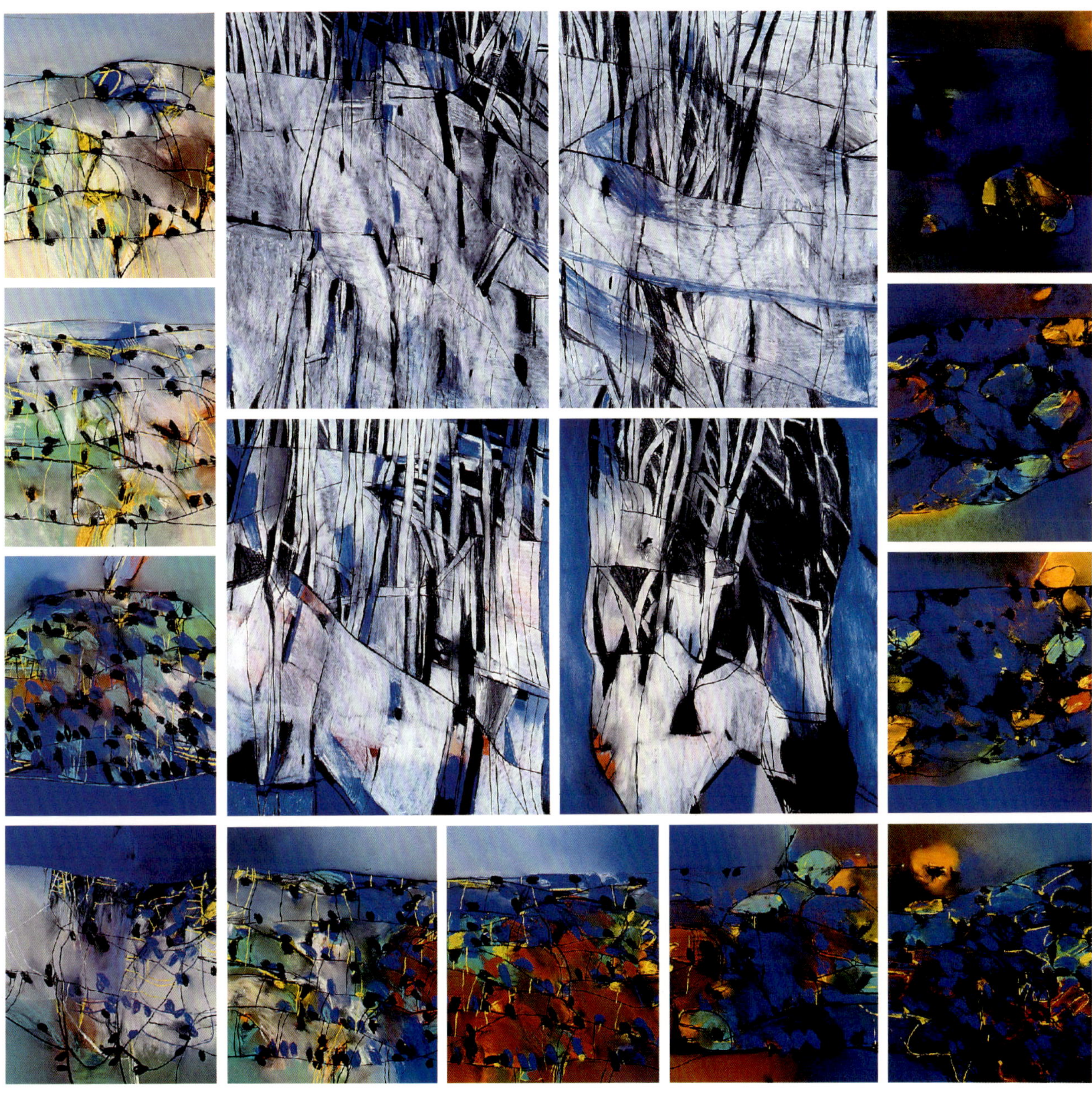

A Landscape Vision No. 7, 1990
Pastel
60" × 65"
Private Collection

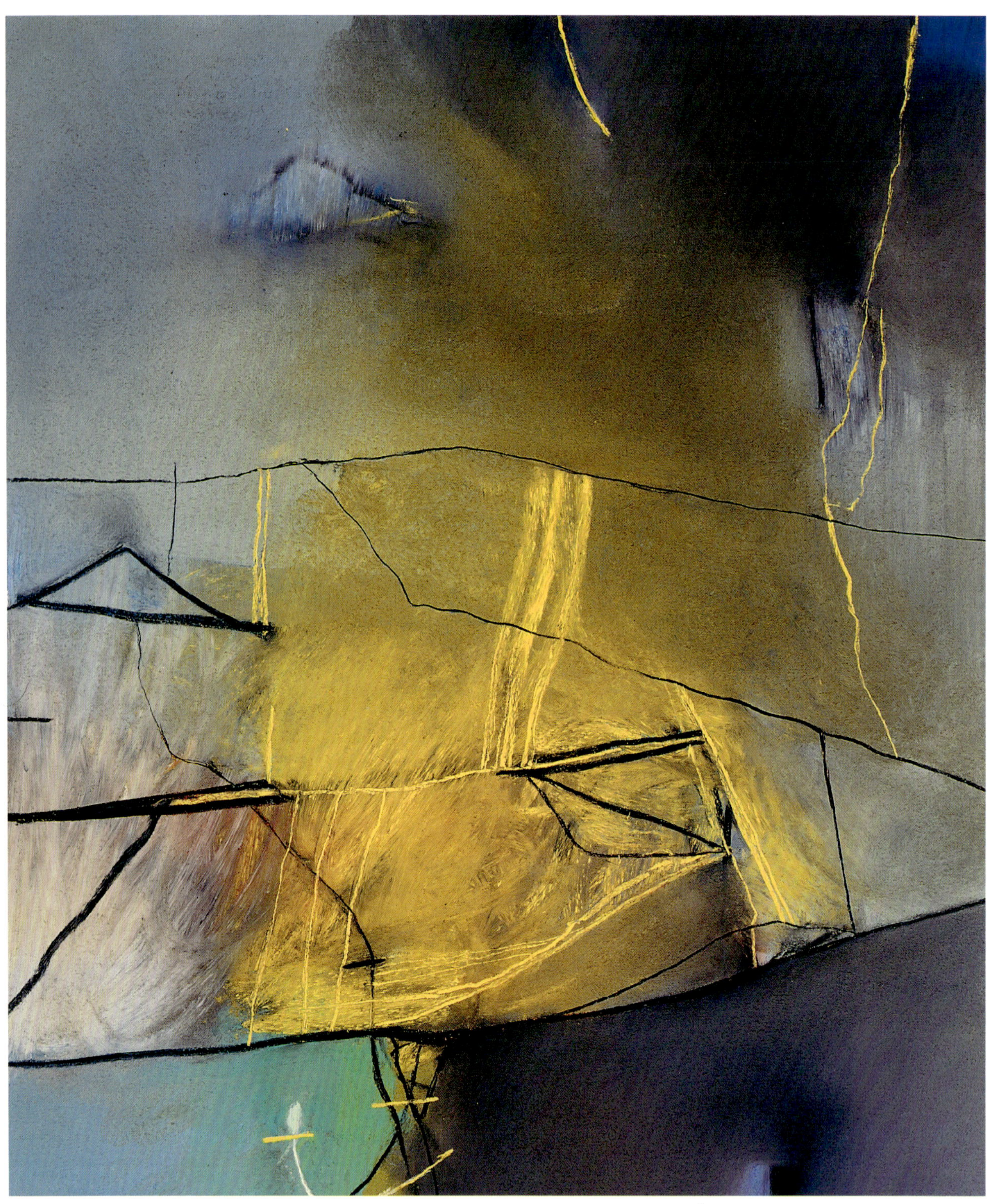

Sunlit Landscape — Peak District, 1991
Pastel
25 1/2" × 21"
Private Collection

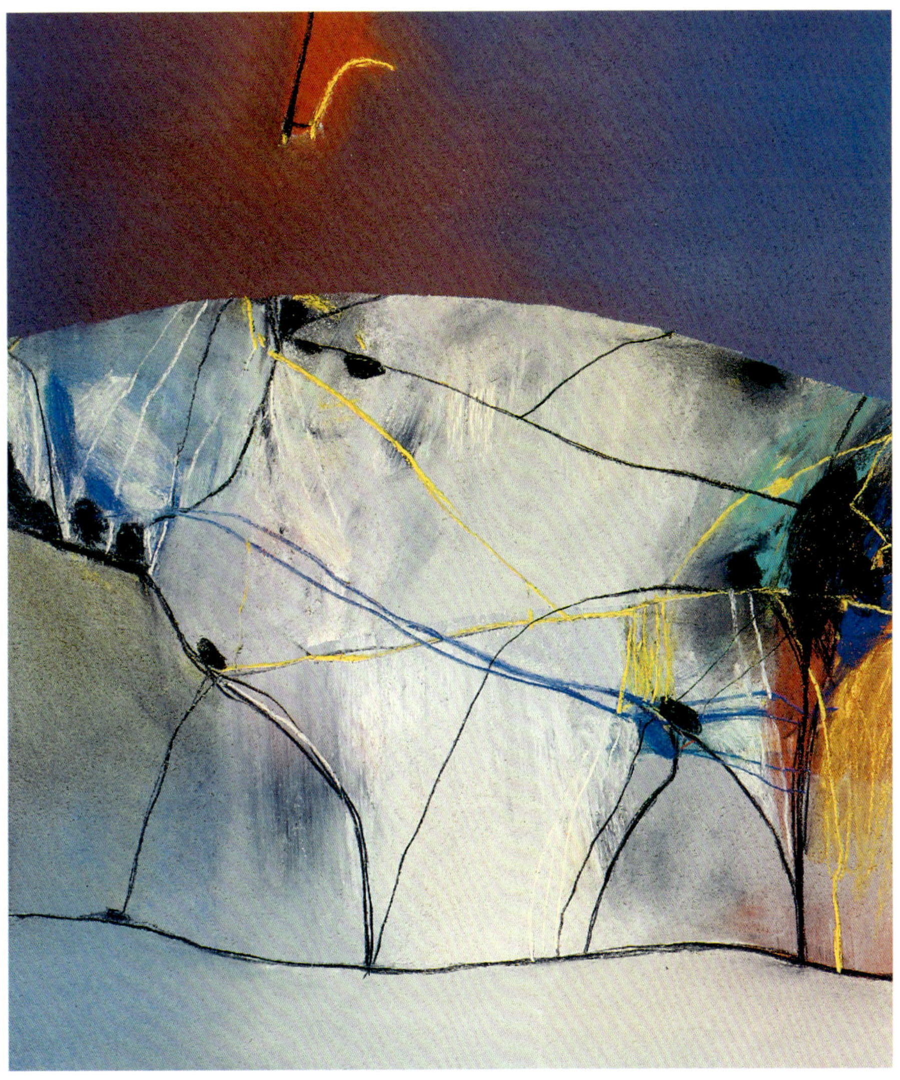

Sunlit Landscape, 1990
Pastel
17" × 14½"
Private Collection

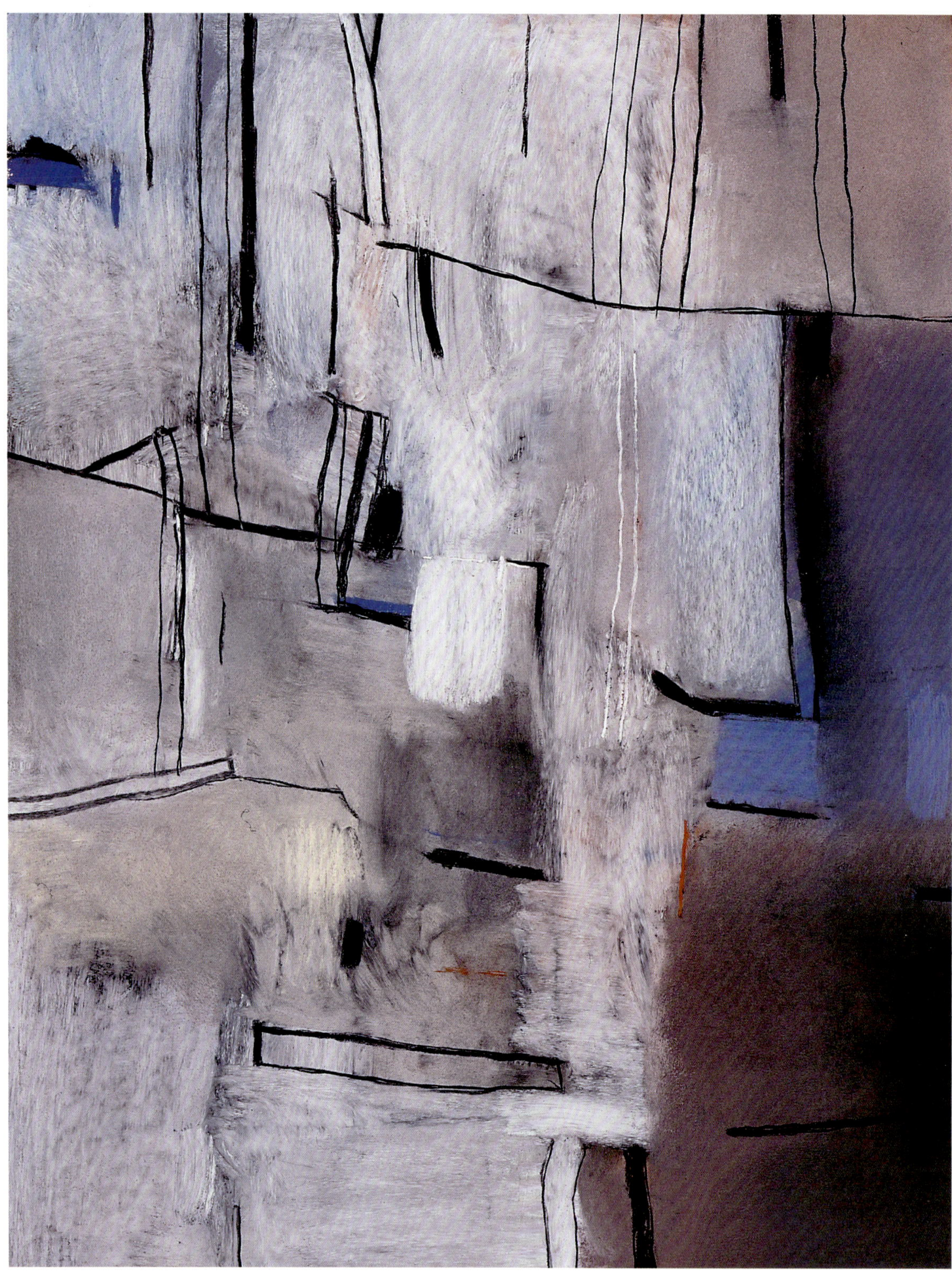

Tree Study — Pale Sunlight, 1990
Pastel
25" × 19"
Private Collection

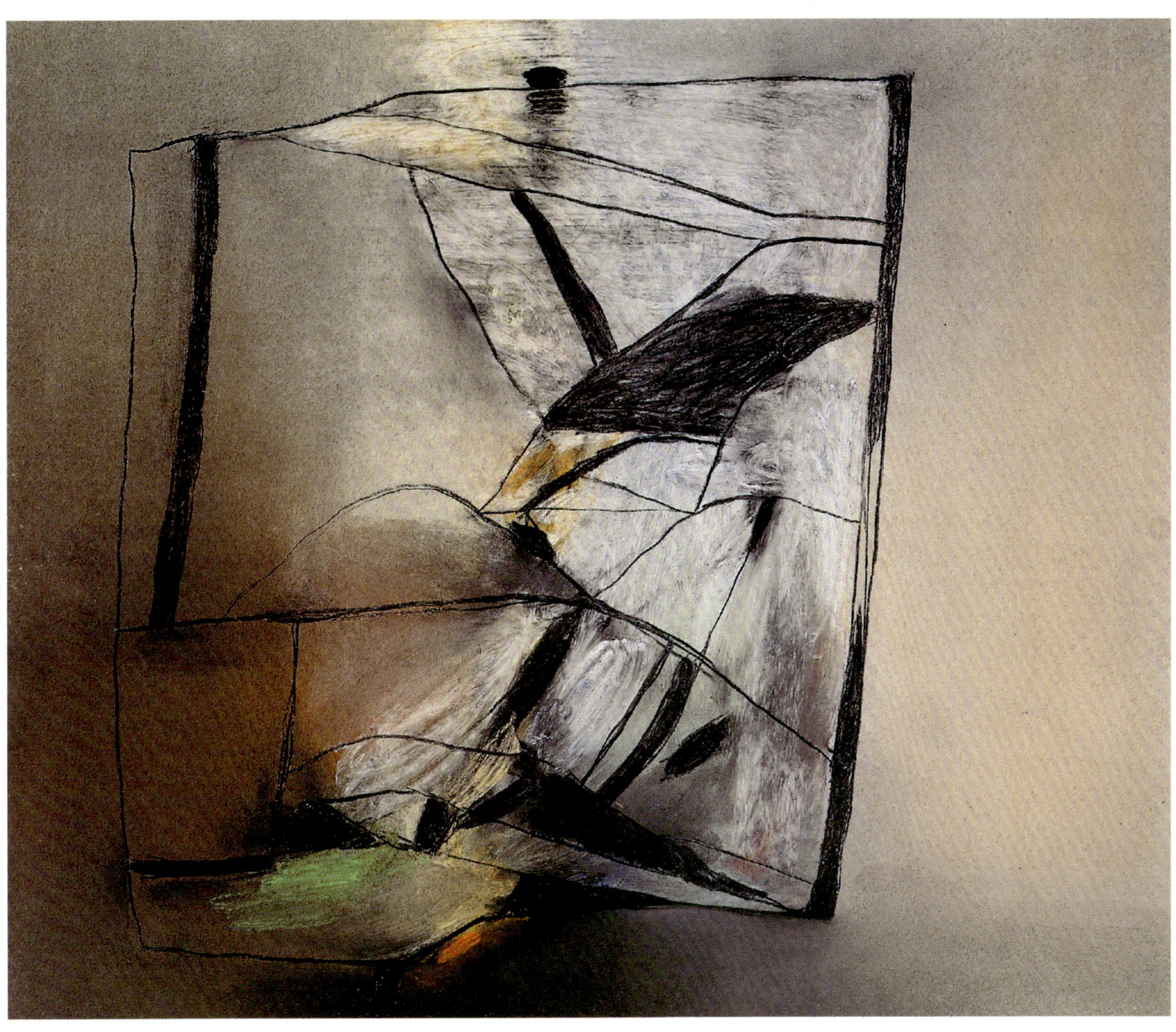

Winter Window, 1991
Pastel
21" × 25"
Private Collection

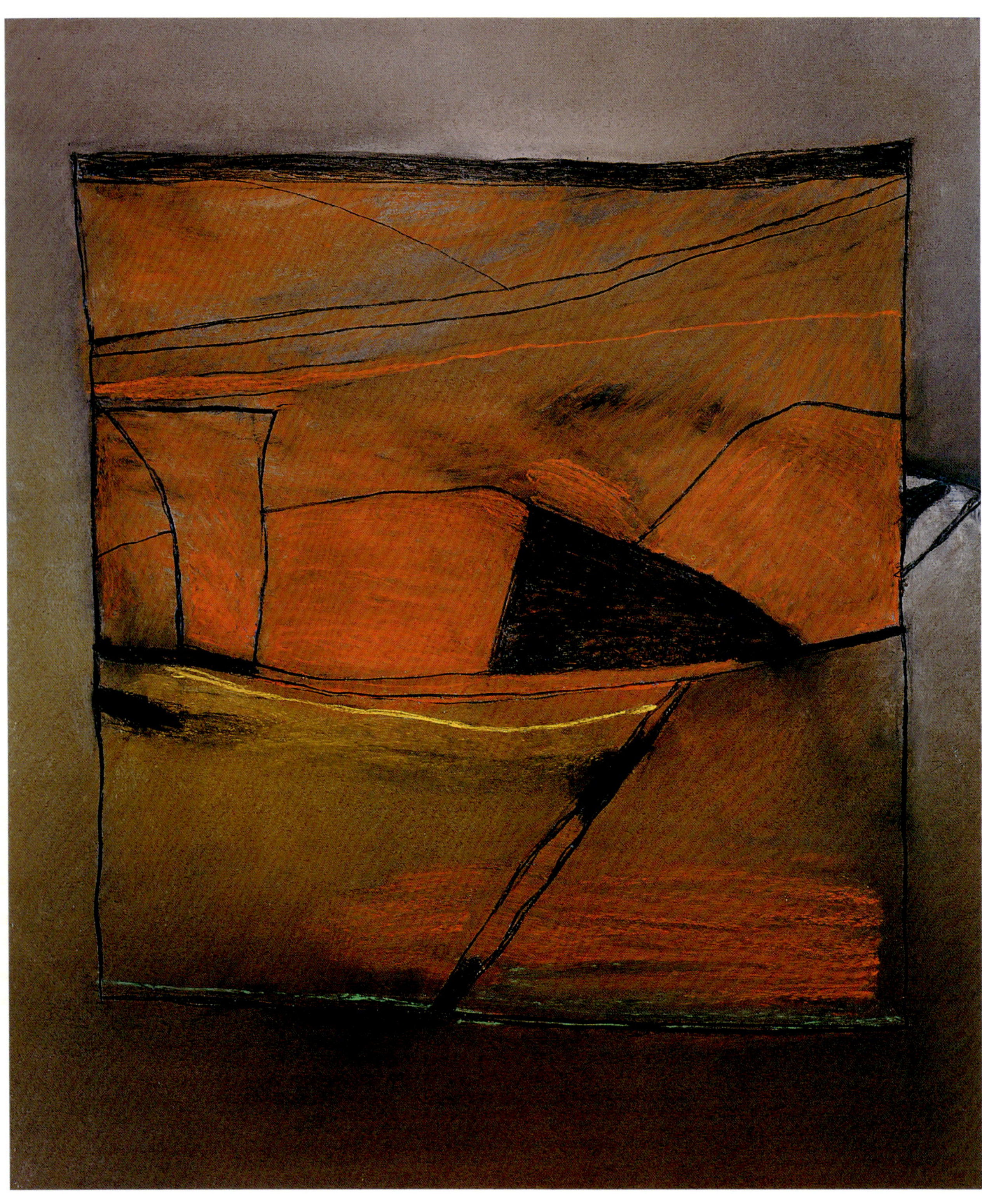

Cooling Towers No. 3, 1991
Pastel
25" × 21"
Private Collection

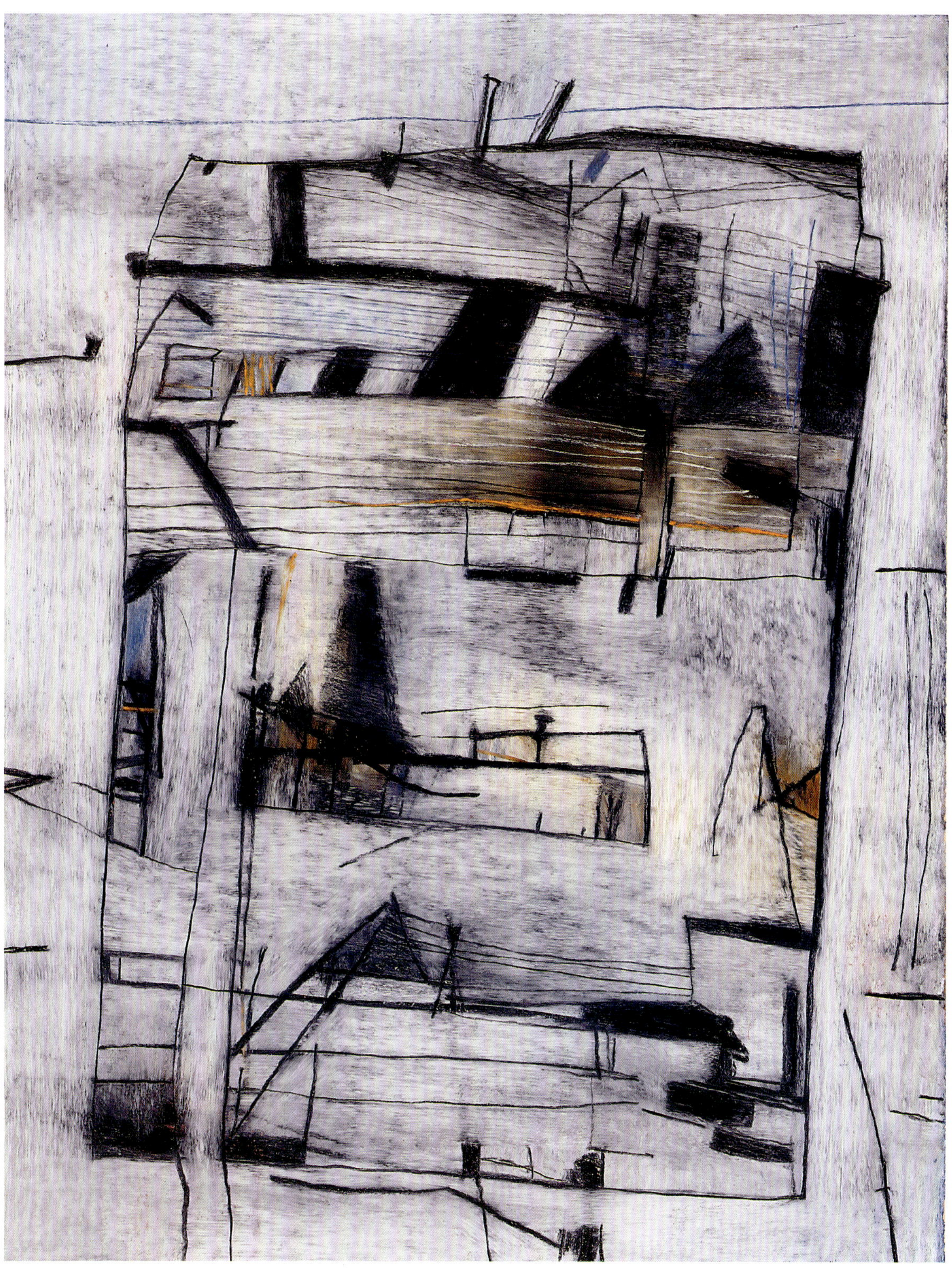

Industrial Shipyard, 1992
Pastel
25" × 19"
Private Collection

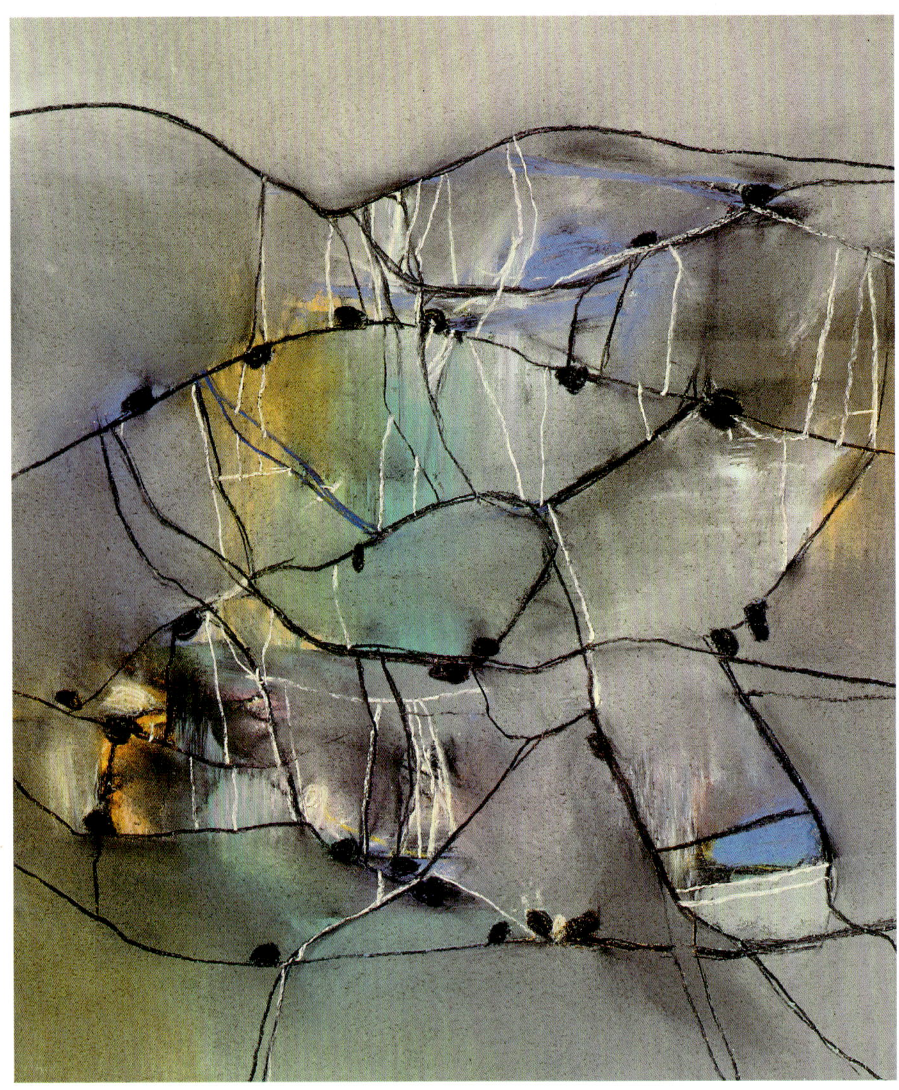

Landscape — Edale, 1990
Pastel
16" × 13½"
Private Collection

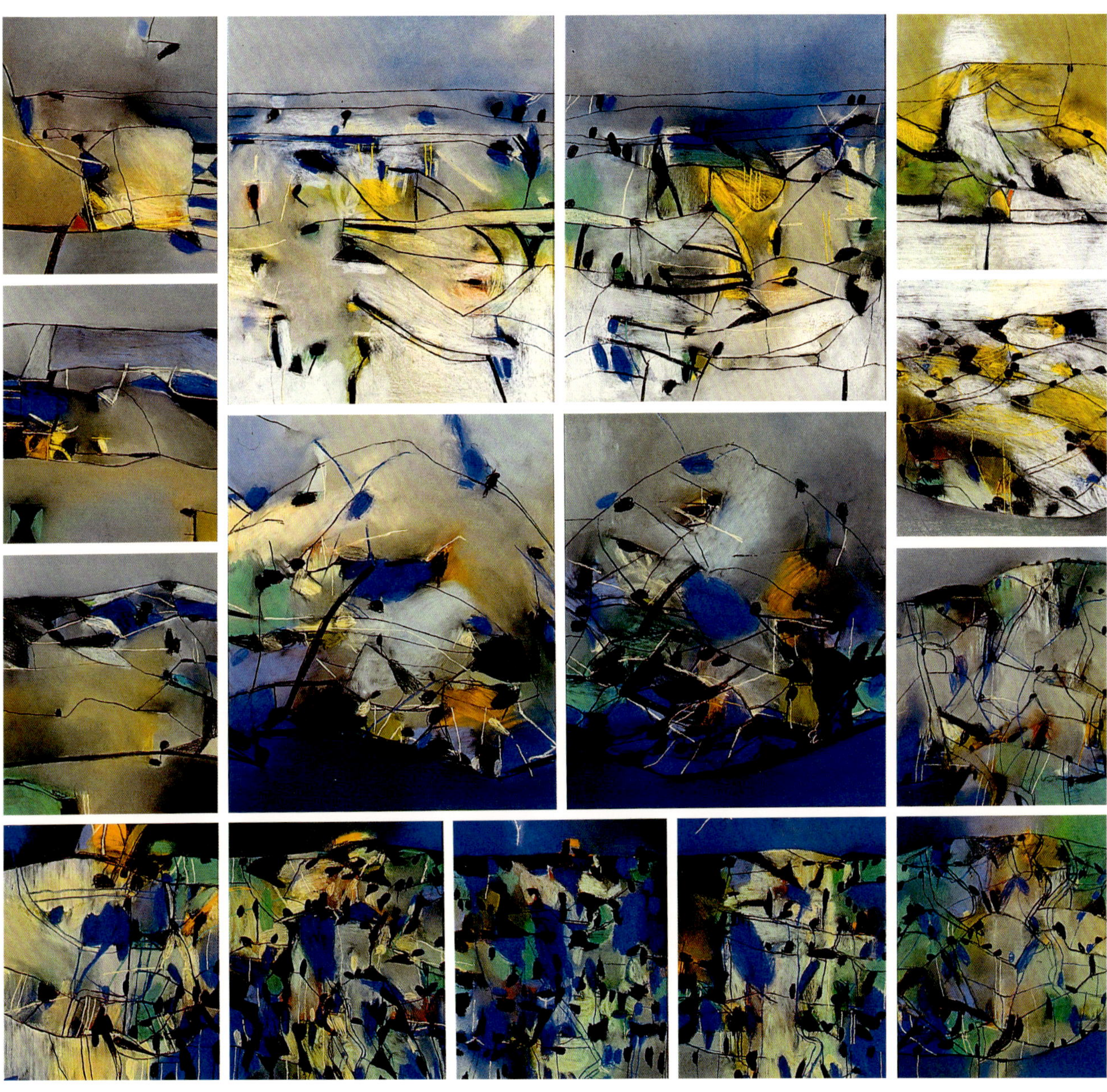

Landscape Vision No. 10, 1991–92
Pastel
63" × 69"
Private Collection

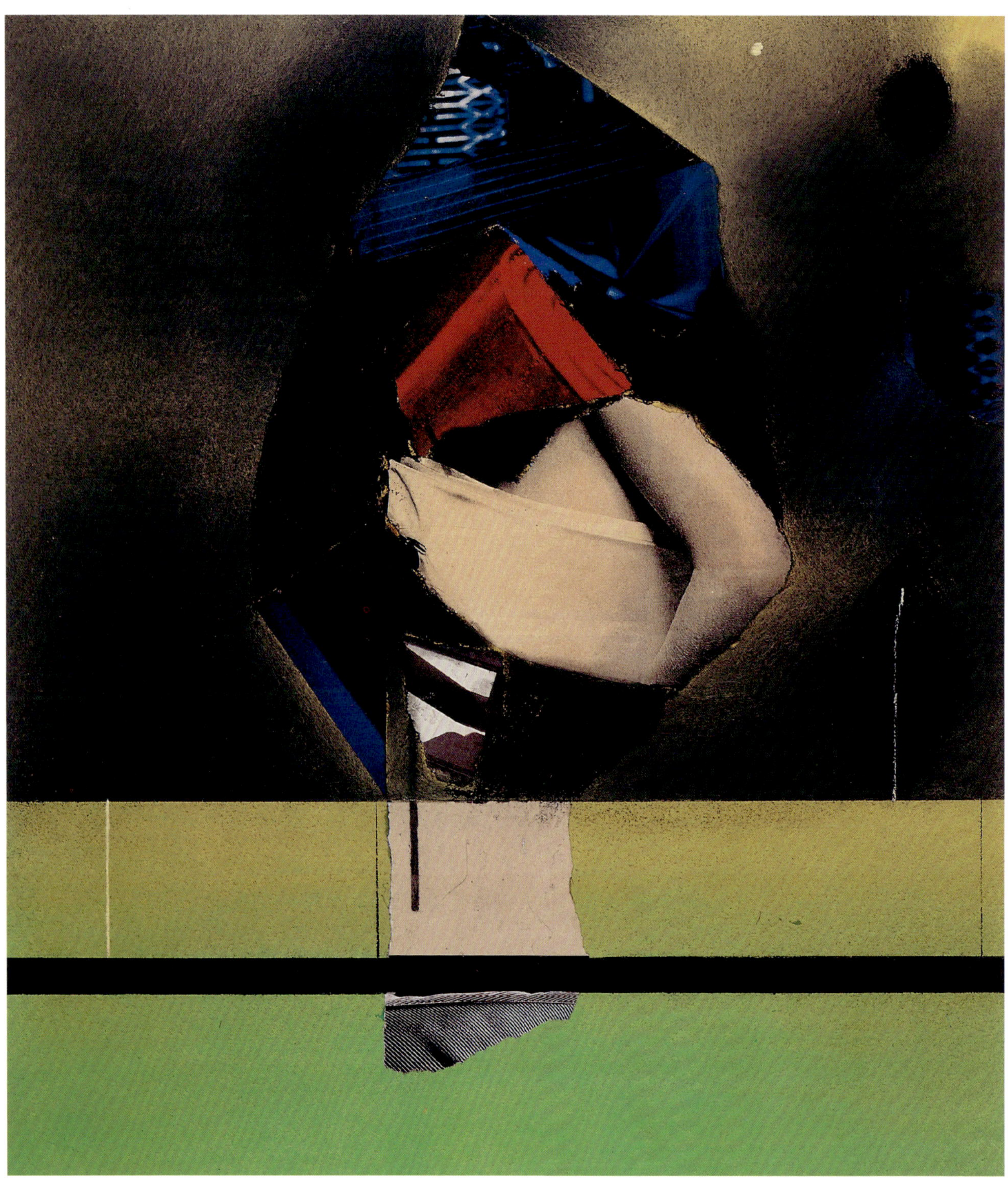

Study, 1992
Pastel & Collage
17" × 15"
Private Collection

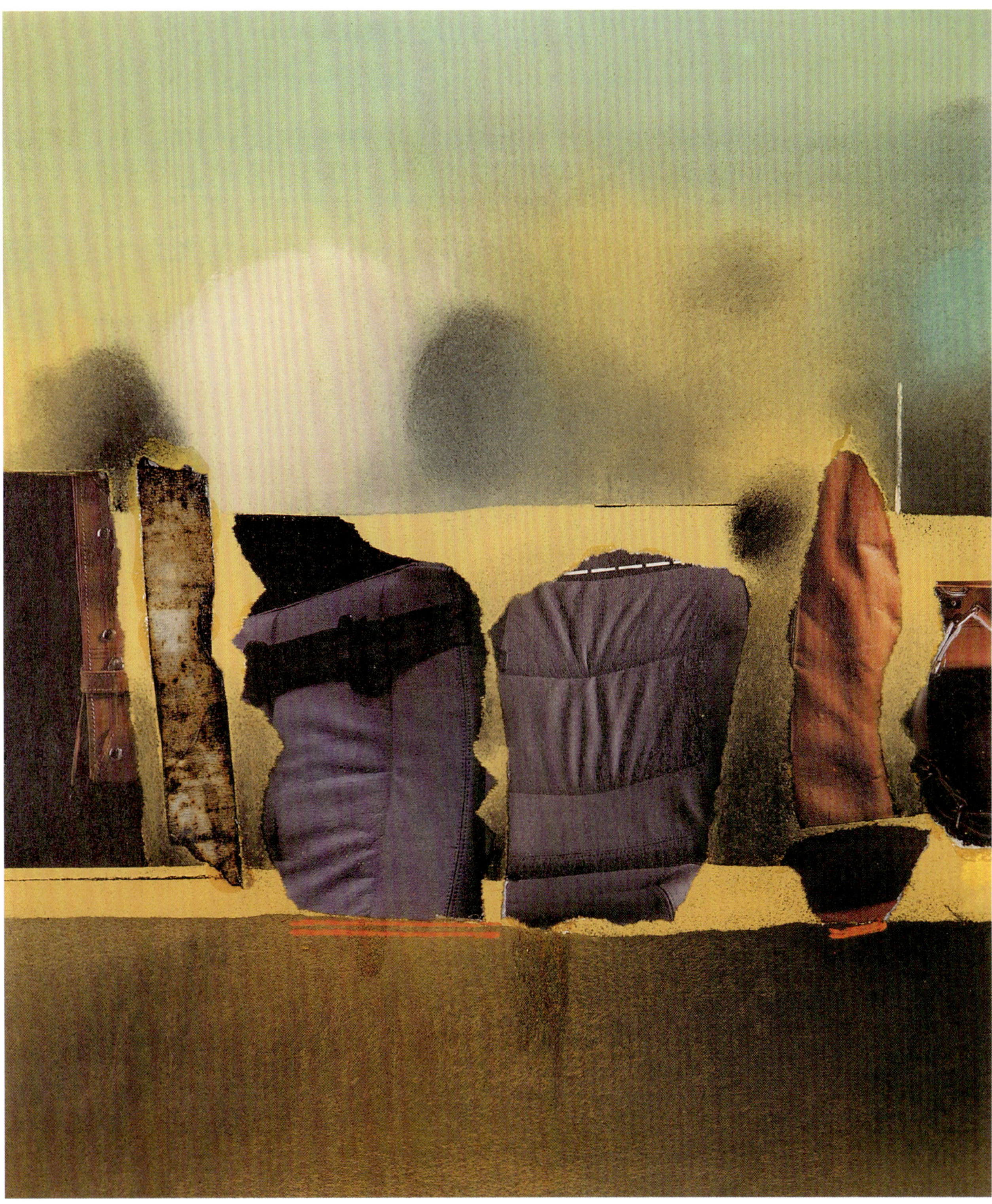

Figurative collage, 1992
Pastel & Collage
16" × 14"

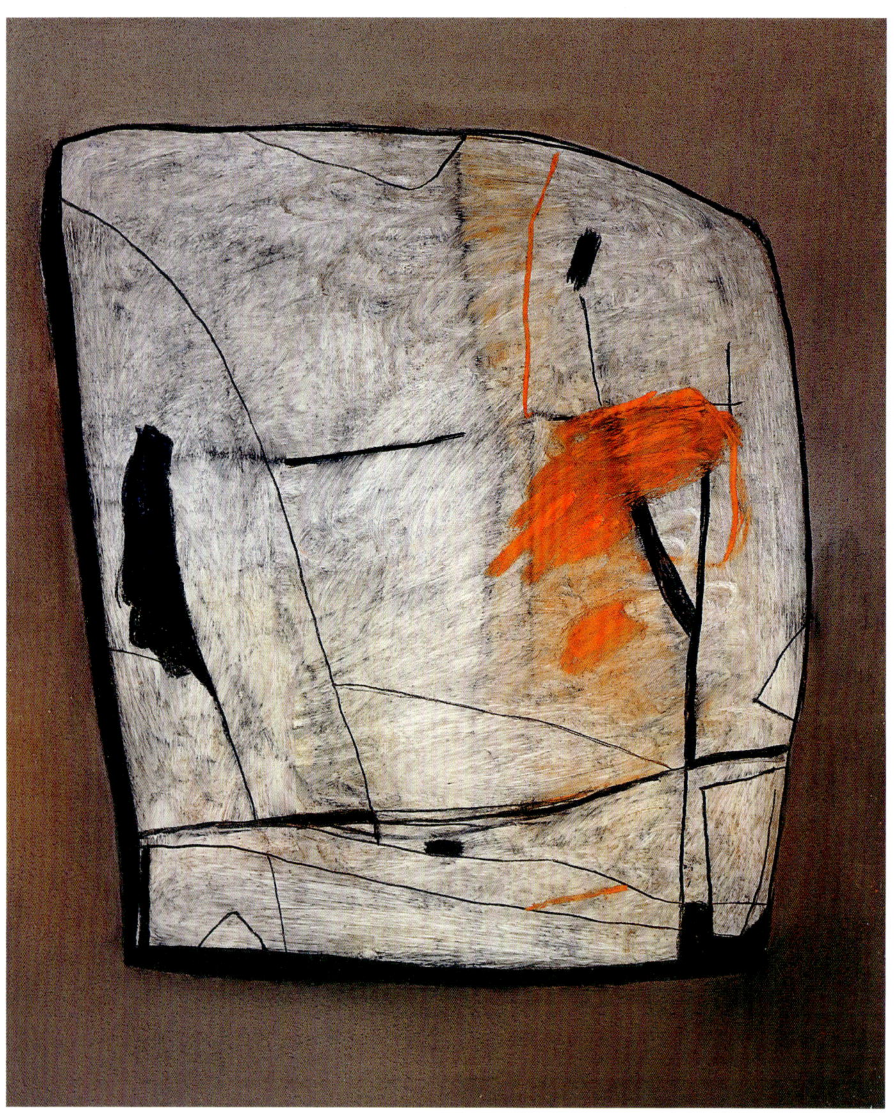

Japanese Tree II, 1993
Pastel
24" × 19"
Private Collection

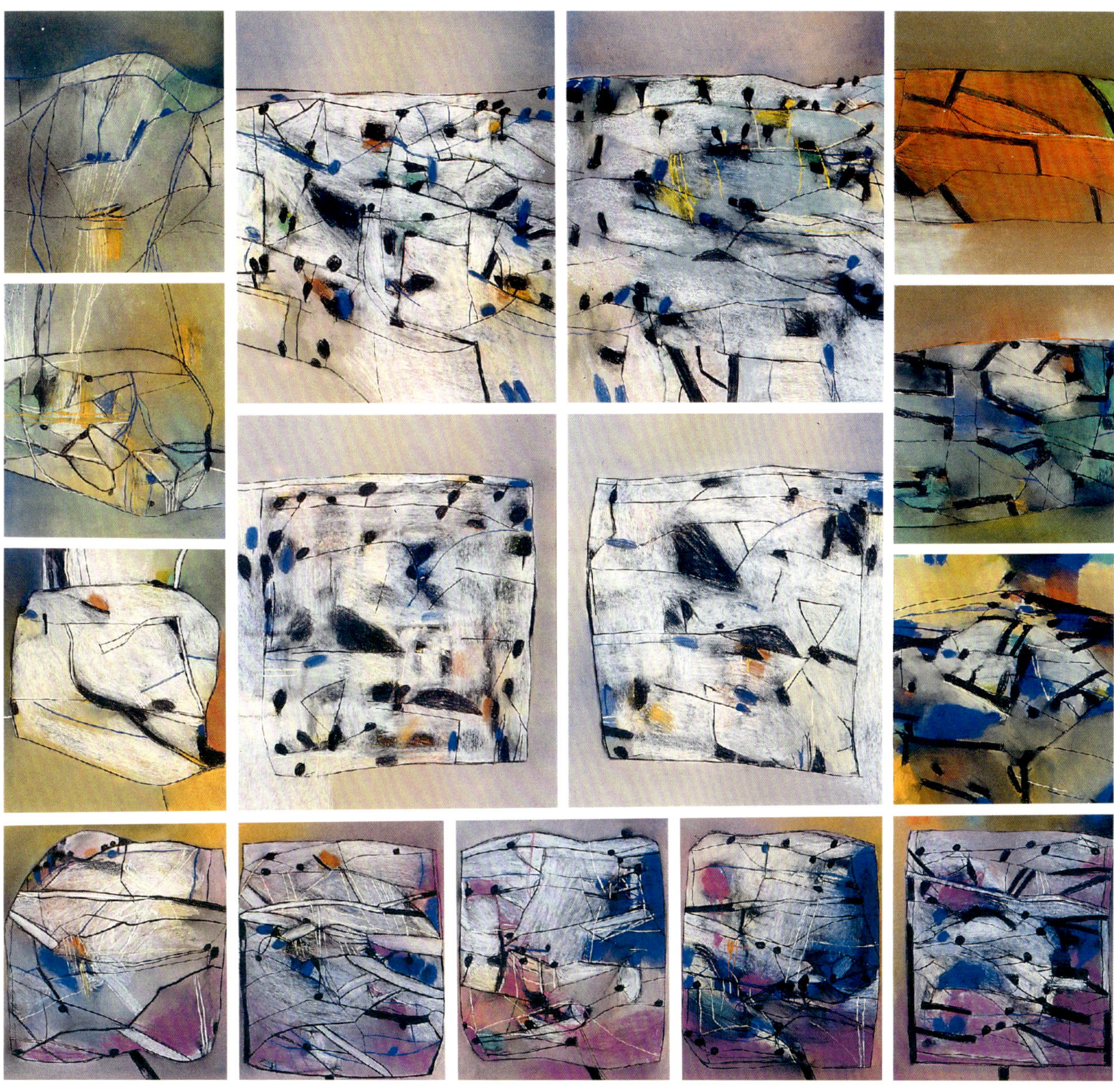

Landscape Vision No. 11, 1992–93
Pastel
64" × 70"
Private Collection

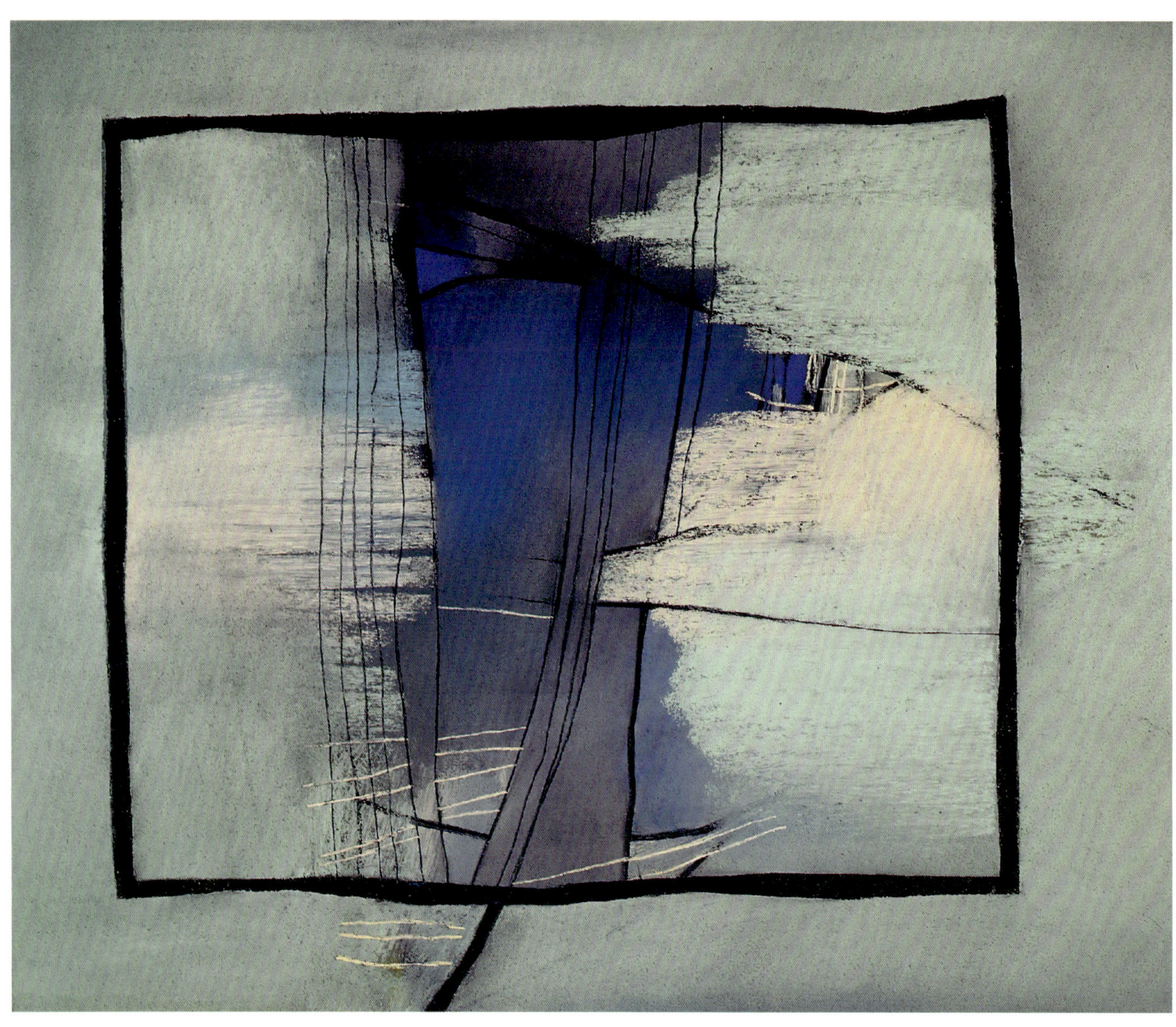

Woodland Window, 1993
Pastel
20" × 24"
Private Collection

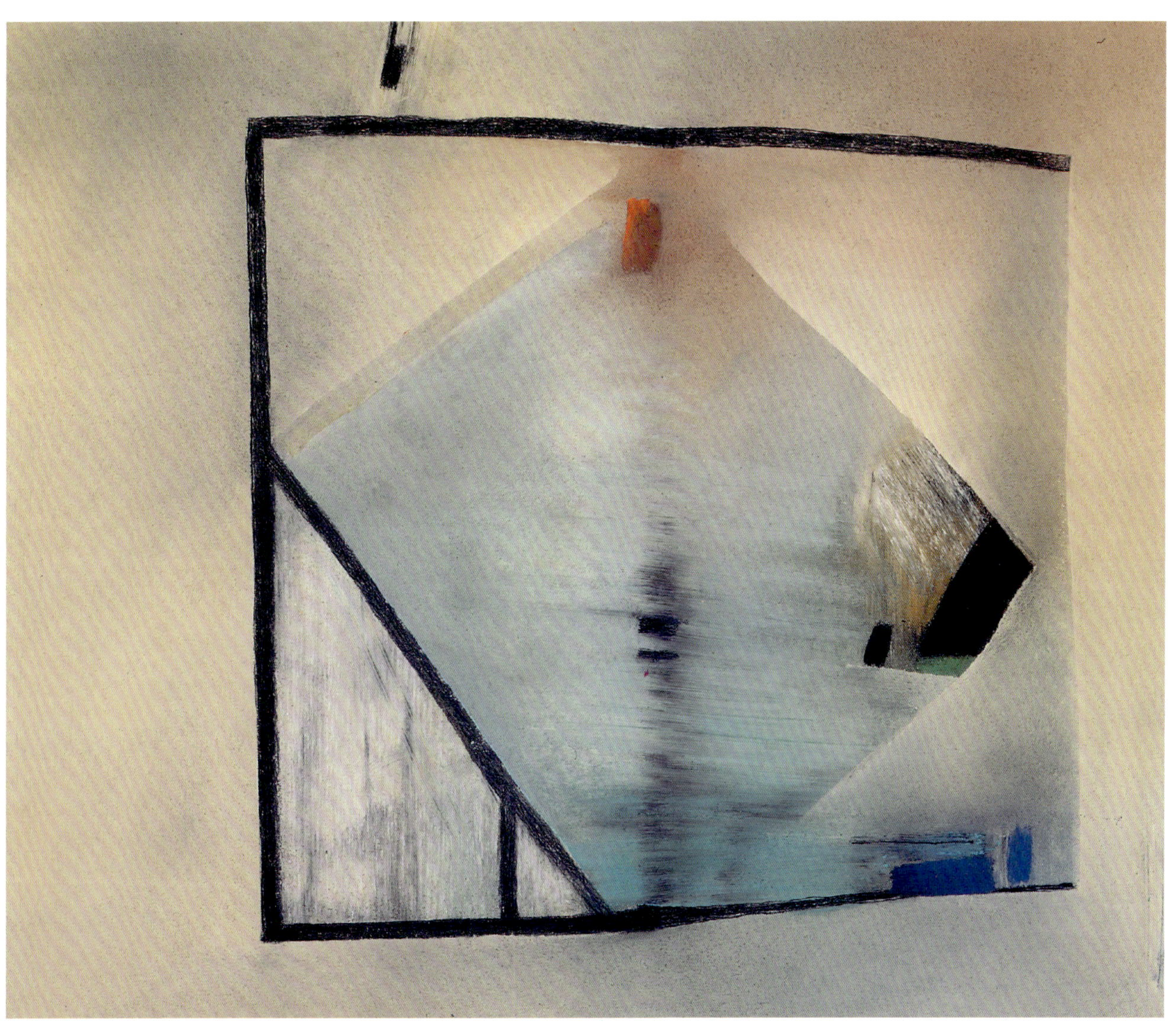

Beach Window, 1993
Pastel
21" × 25"
Private Collection

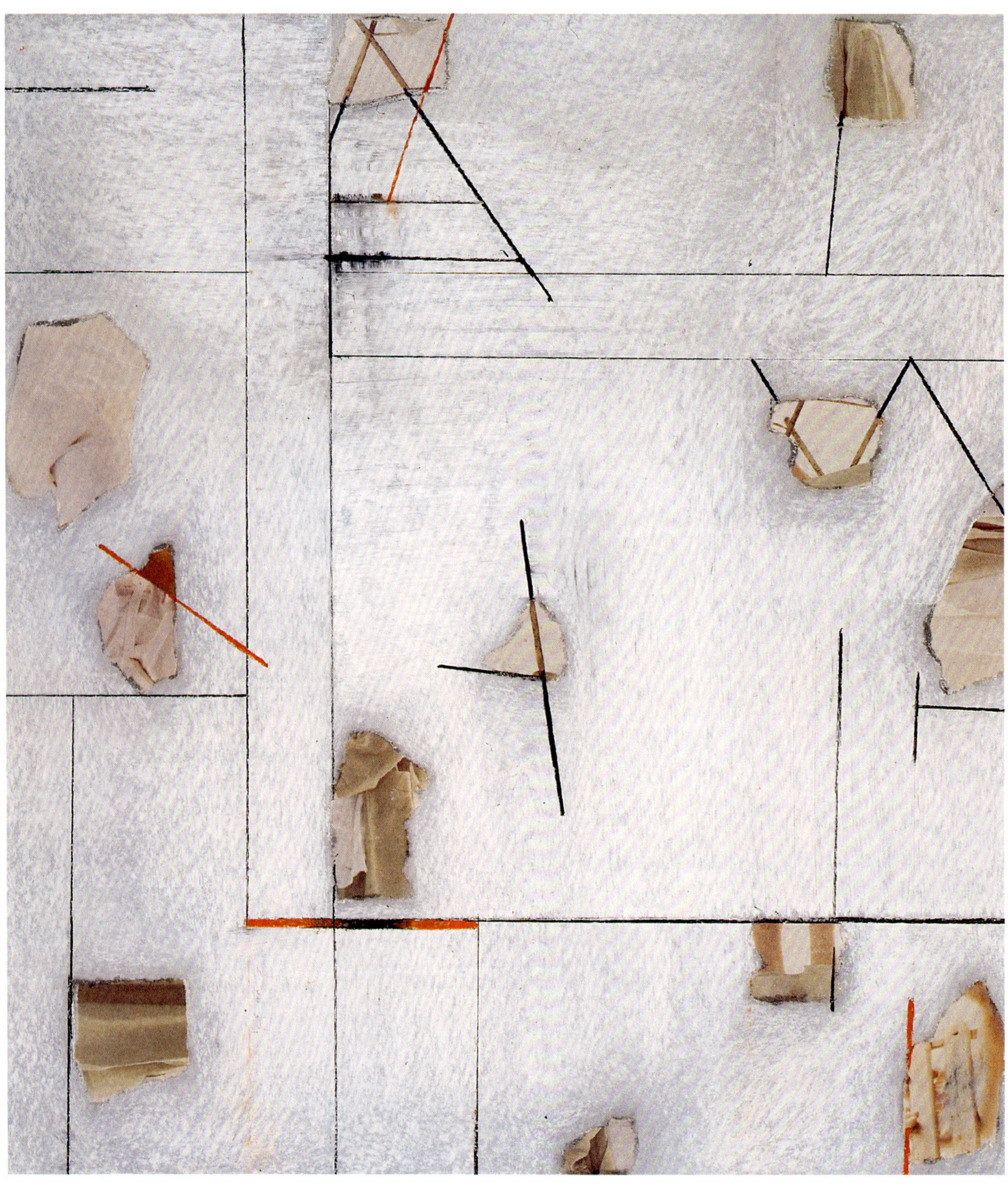

White Collage, 1993
Pastel & Collage
17" × 15"

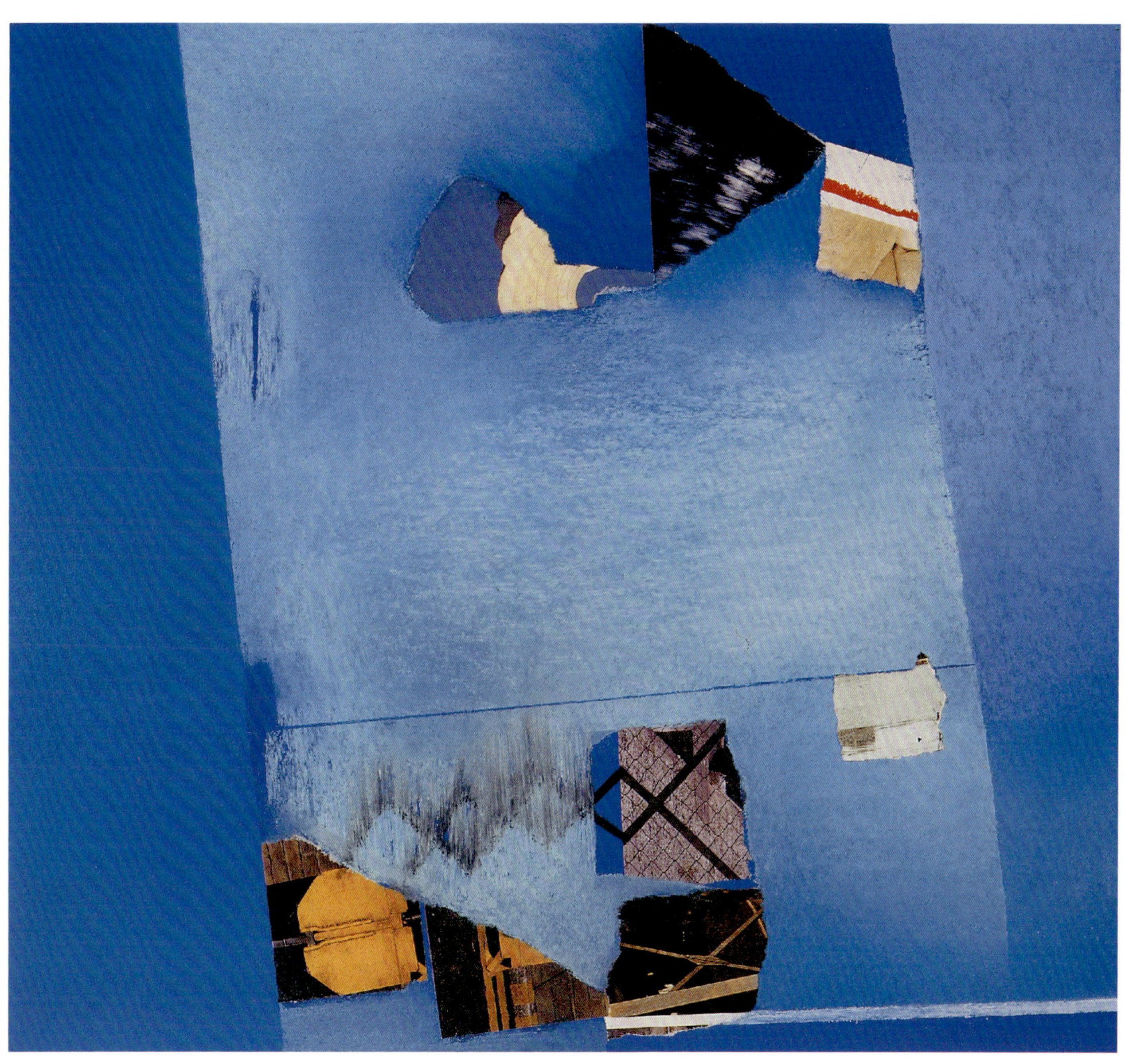

Cliff Blue, 1993
Pastel & Collage
15" × 17"

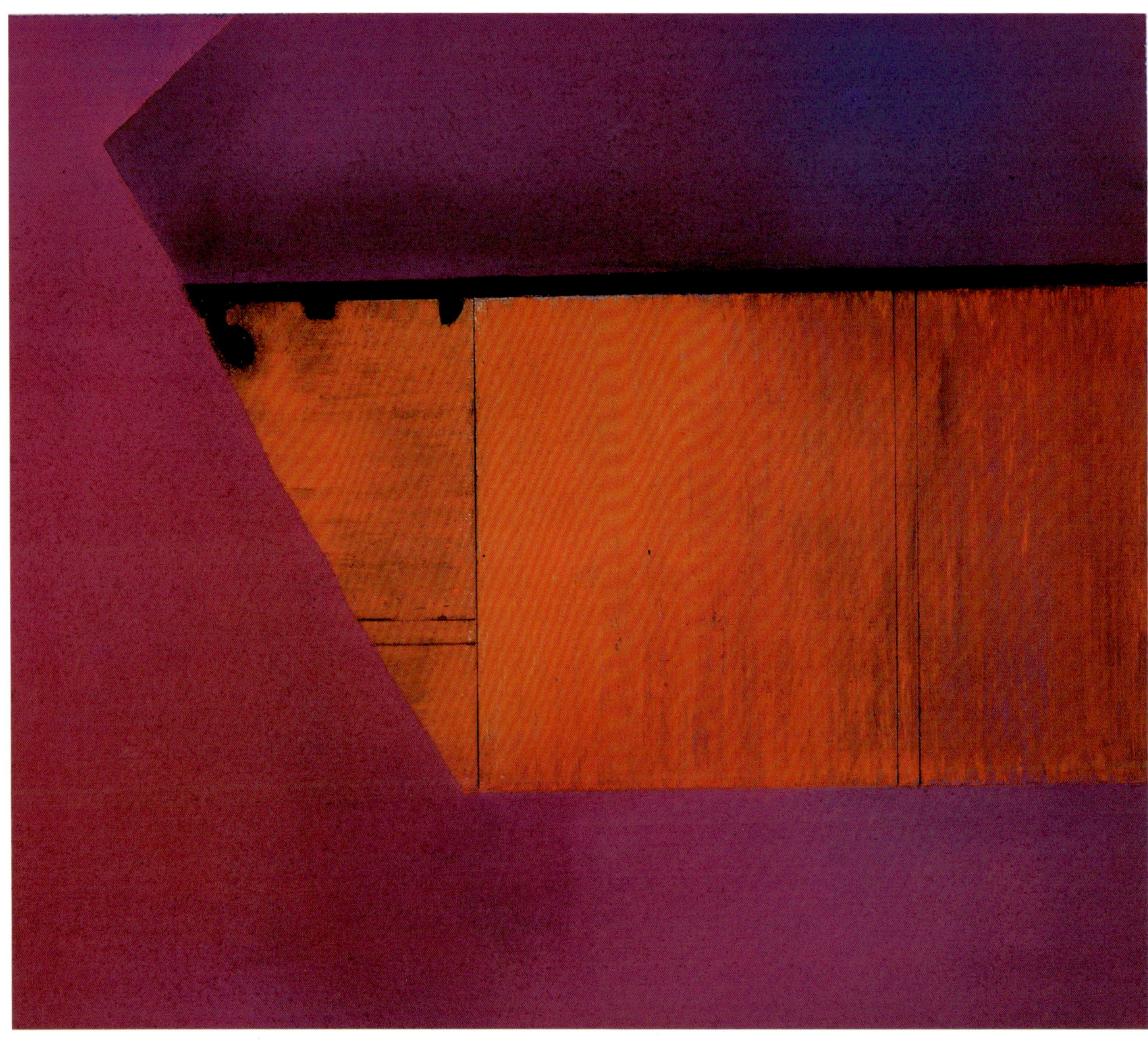

Sunset Wheatfields, 1993
Pastel
14 1/2" × 16"
Private Collection

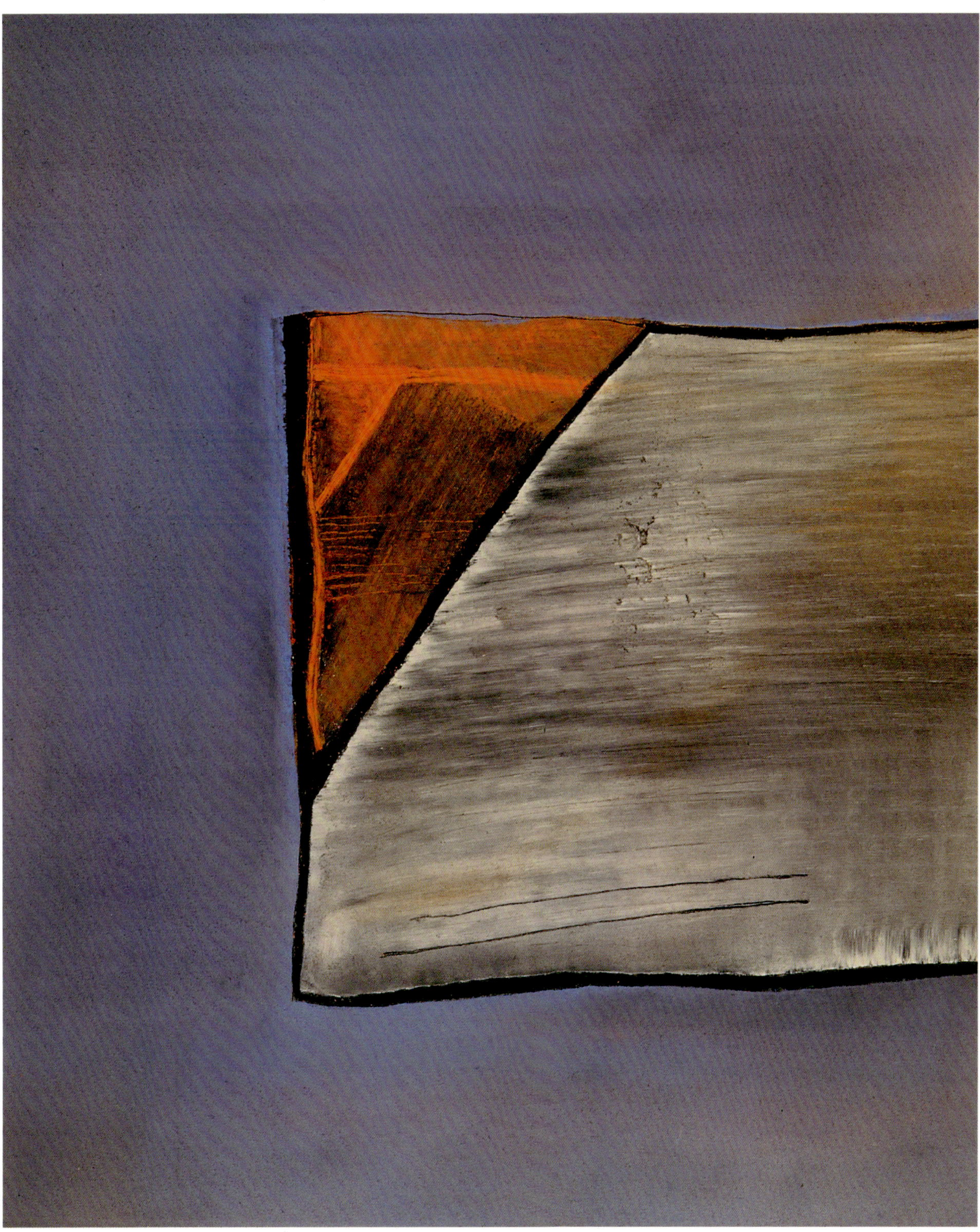

Blue and Orange, 1993
Pastel
25" × 21"
Private Collection

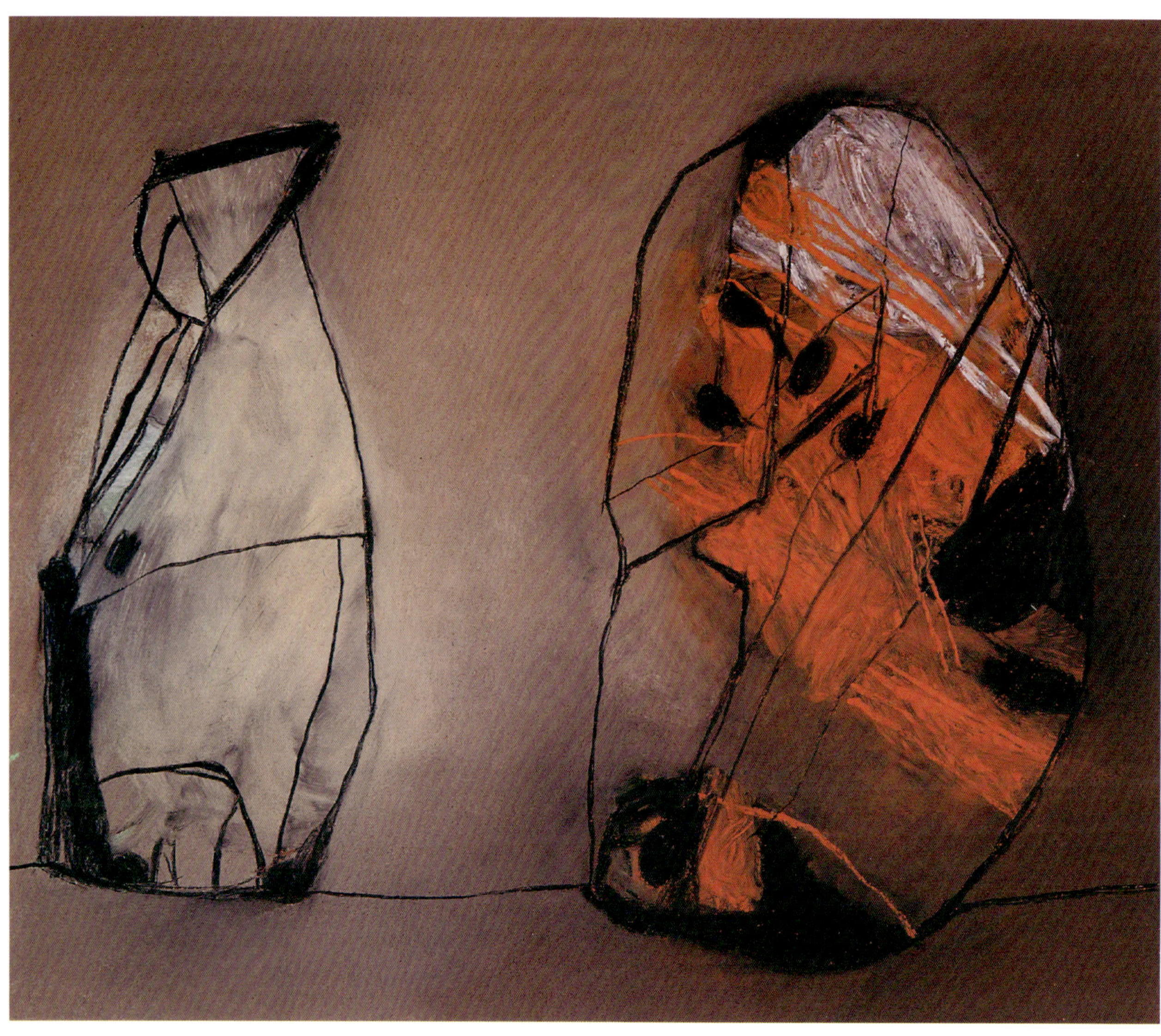

Stones and Sunset, 1993
Pastel
14 1/4" × 17"
Private Collection

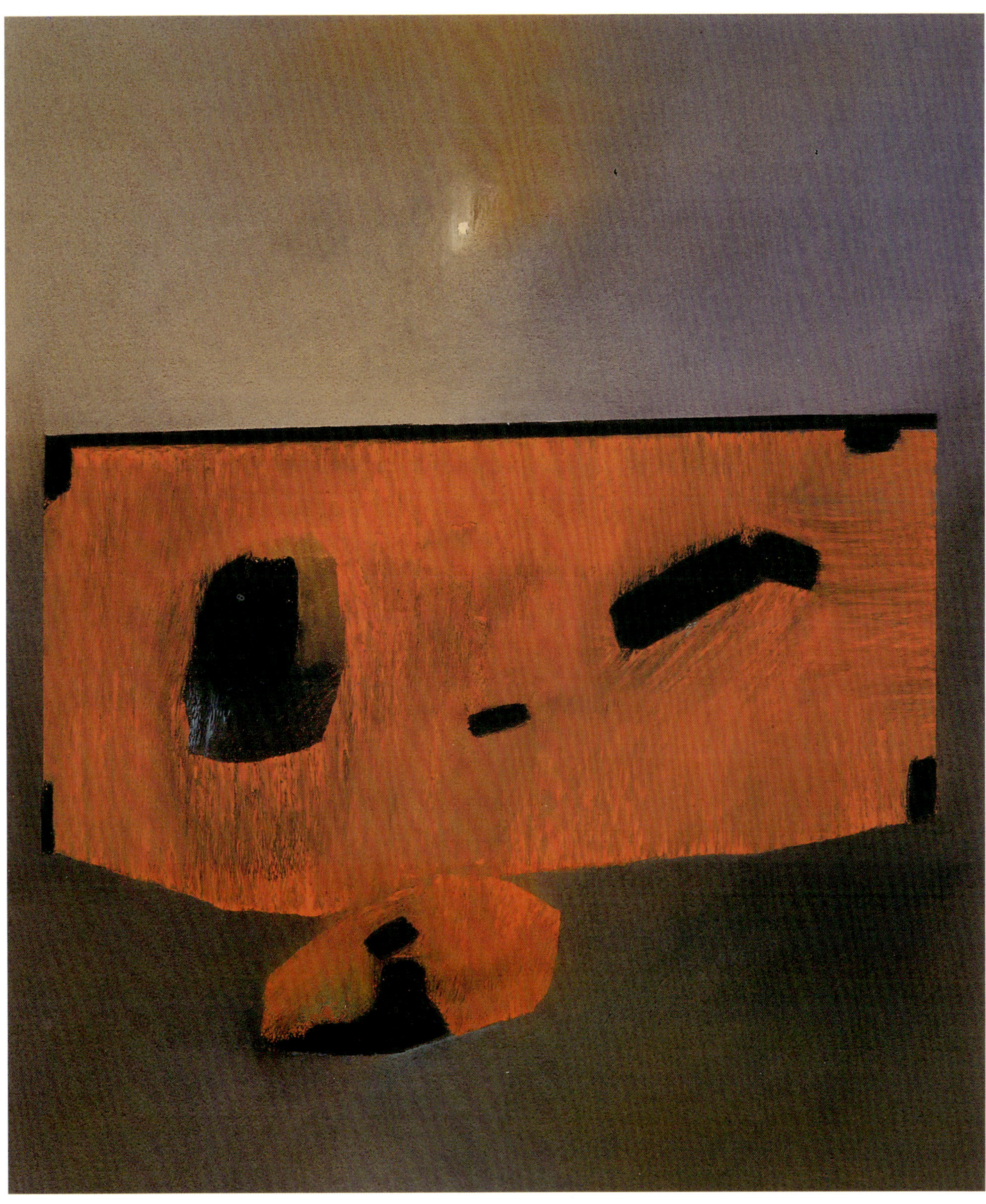

Stones and Canadian Wheatfields, 1993
Pastel
24" × 20"
Private Collection

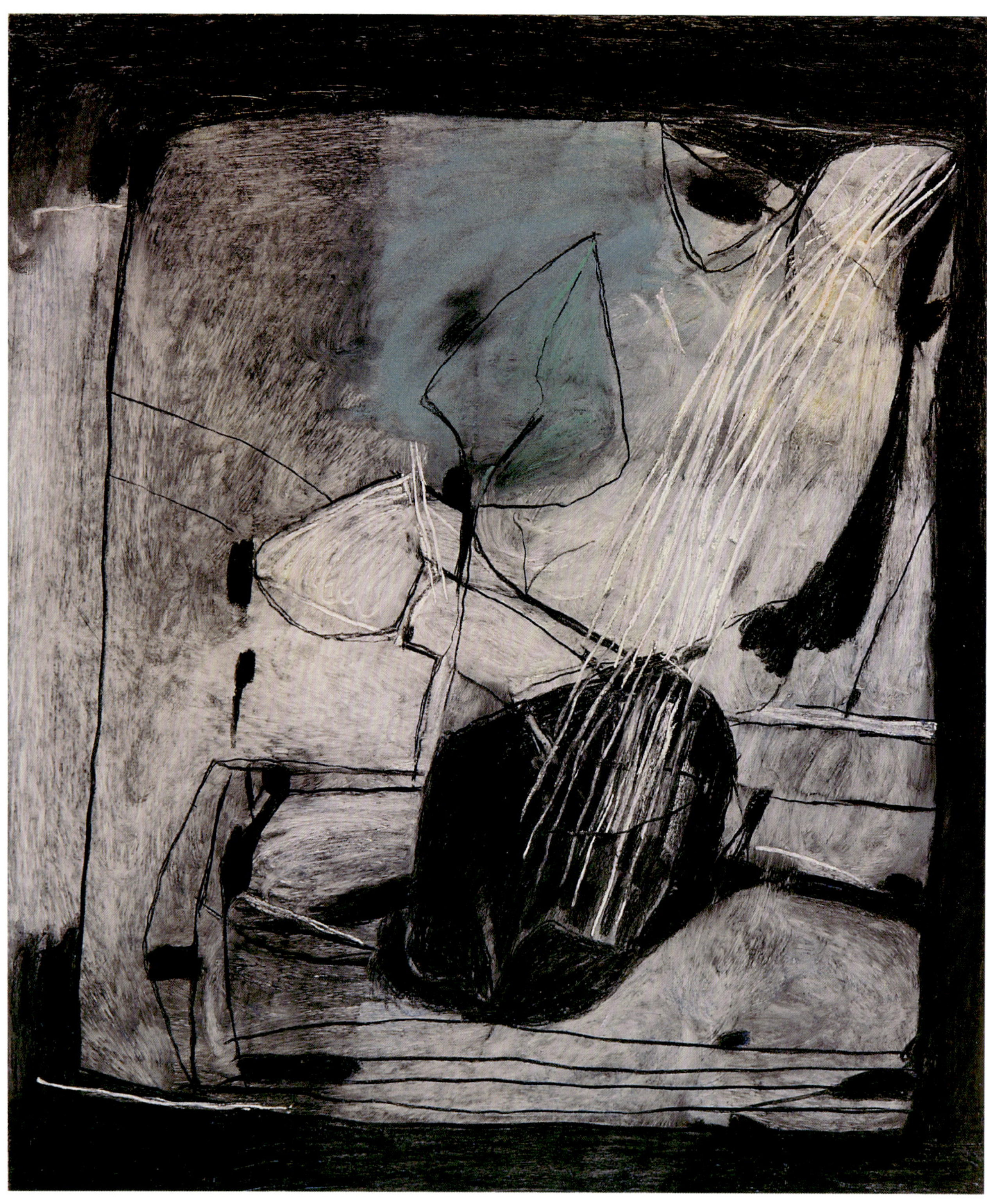

Mystic Stone, 1993
Pastel
24" × 20"
Private Collection

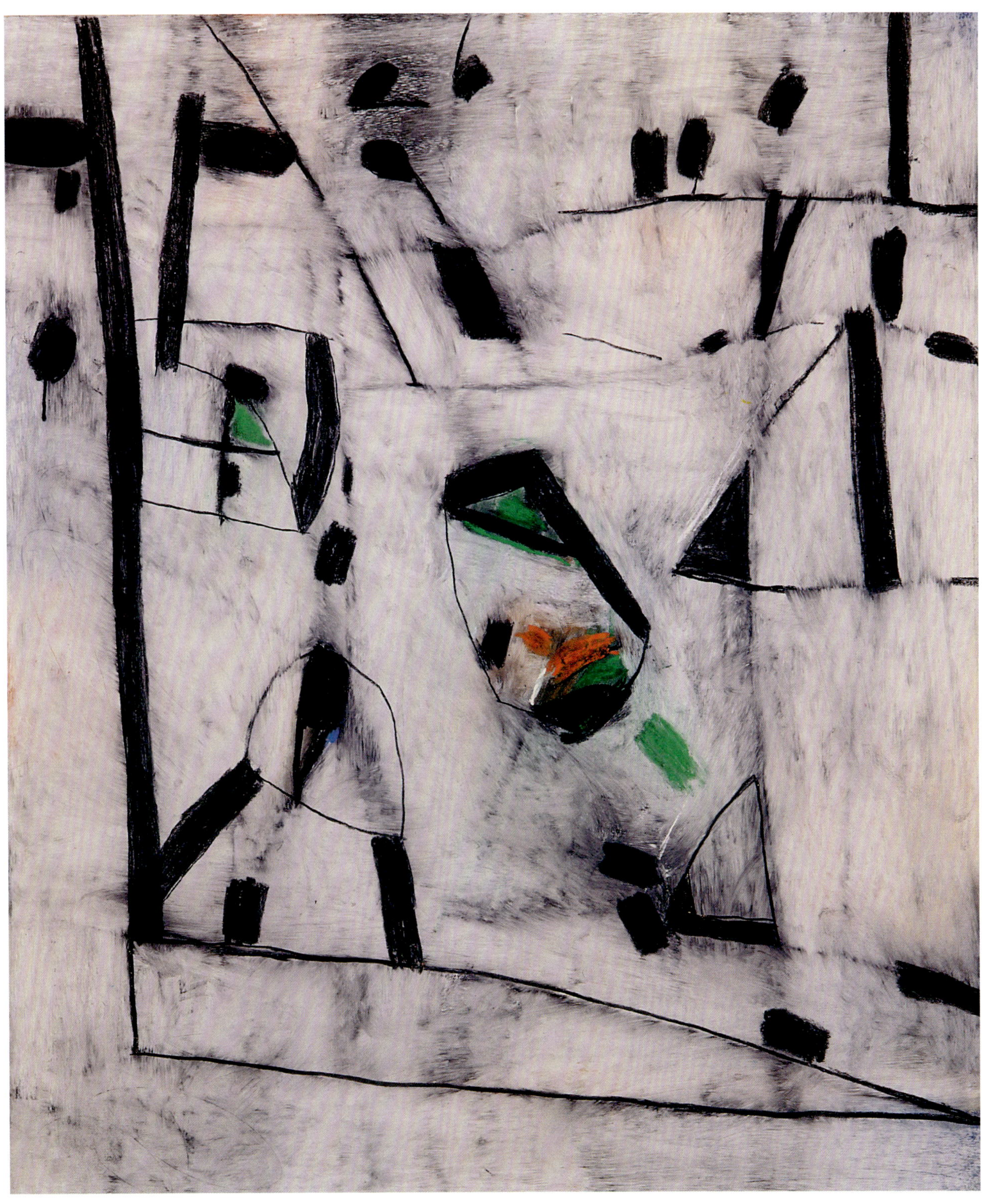

Winter Stones, 1993
Pastel
25" × 21"
Private Collection

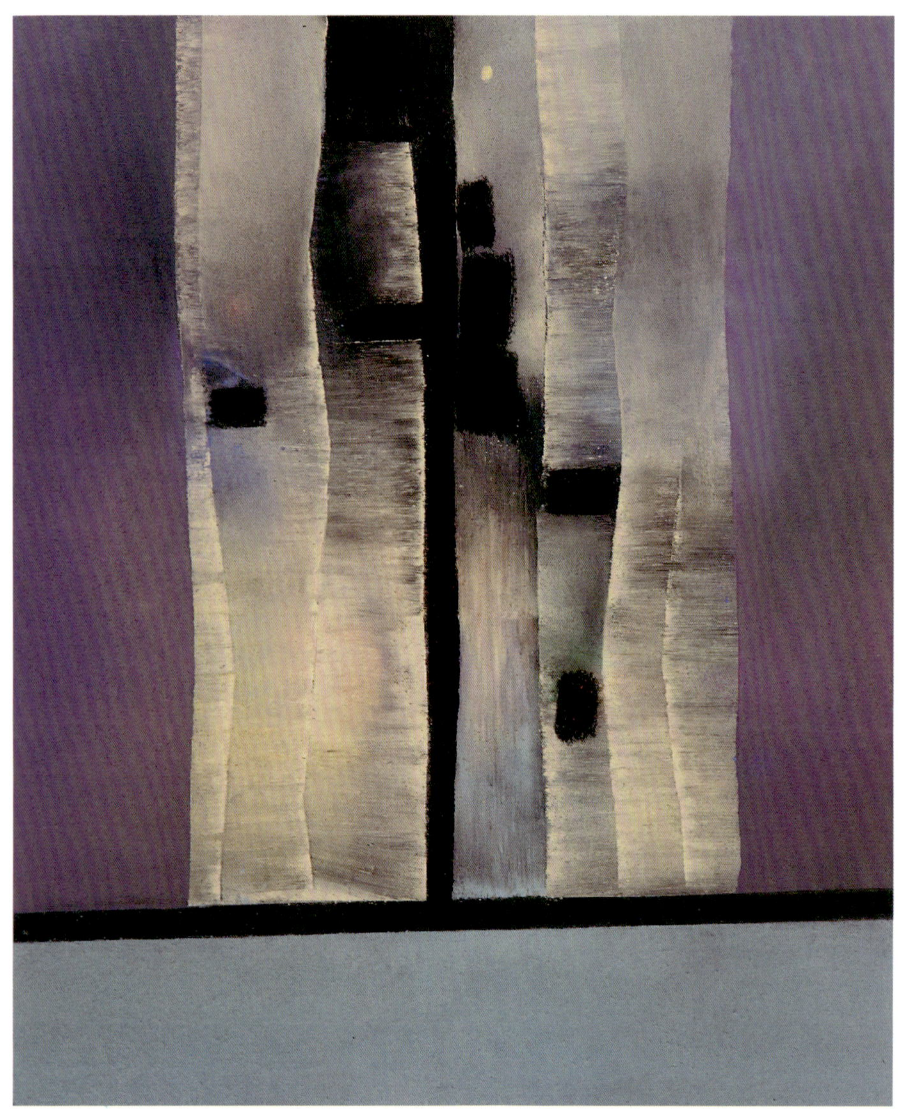

Mystical Tree (study for Landscape Vision, No. 14), 1994
Pastel
17" × 14 1/4"

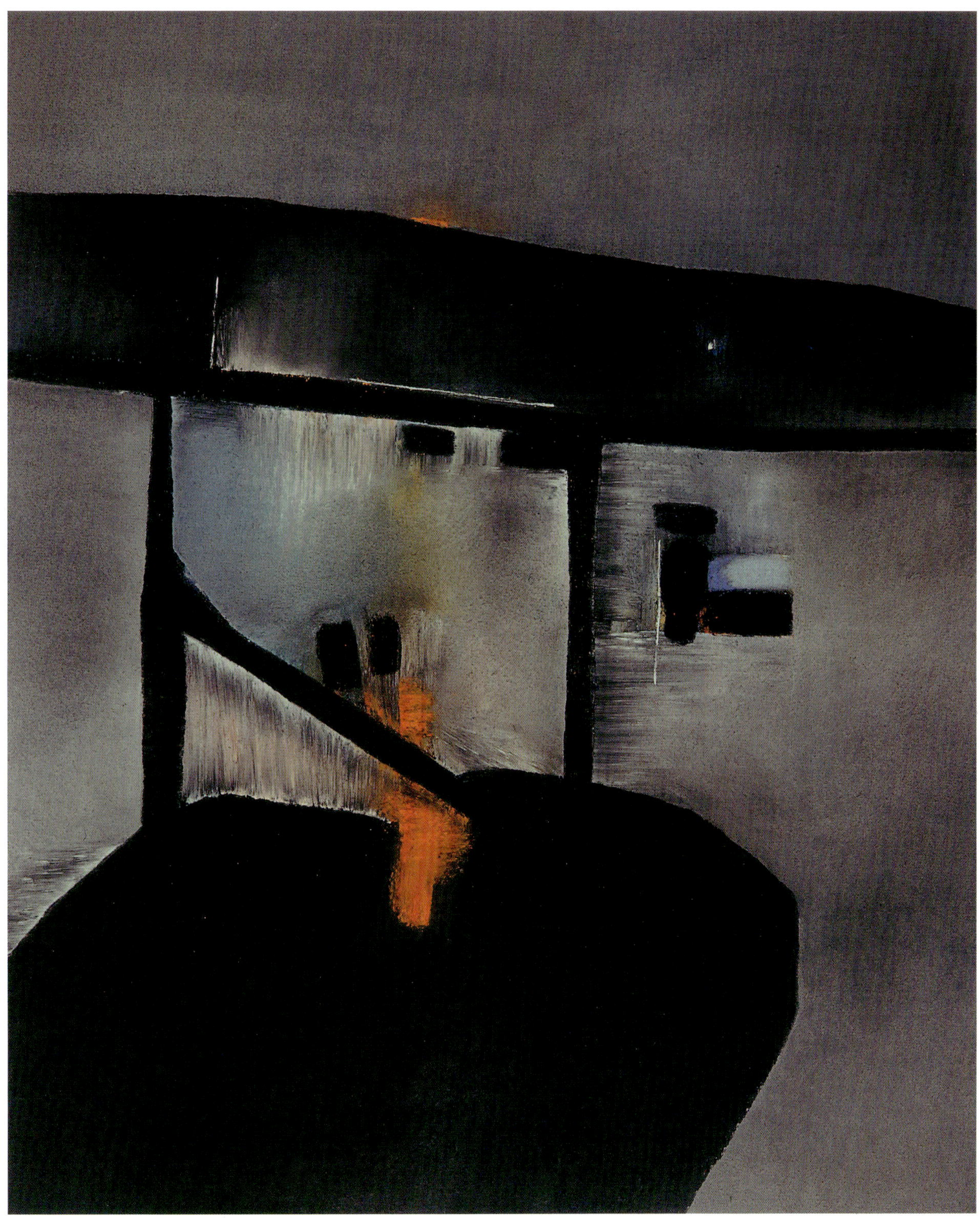

Dark Pool — Sunset, 1994
Pastel
24" × 20"
Private Collection

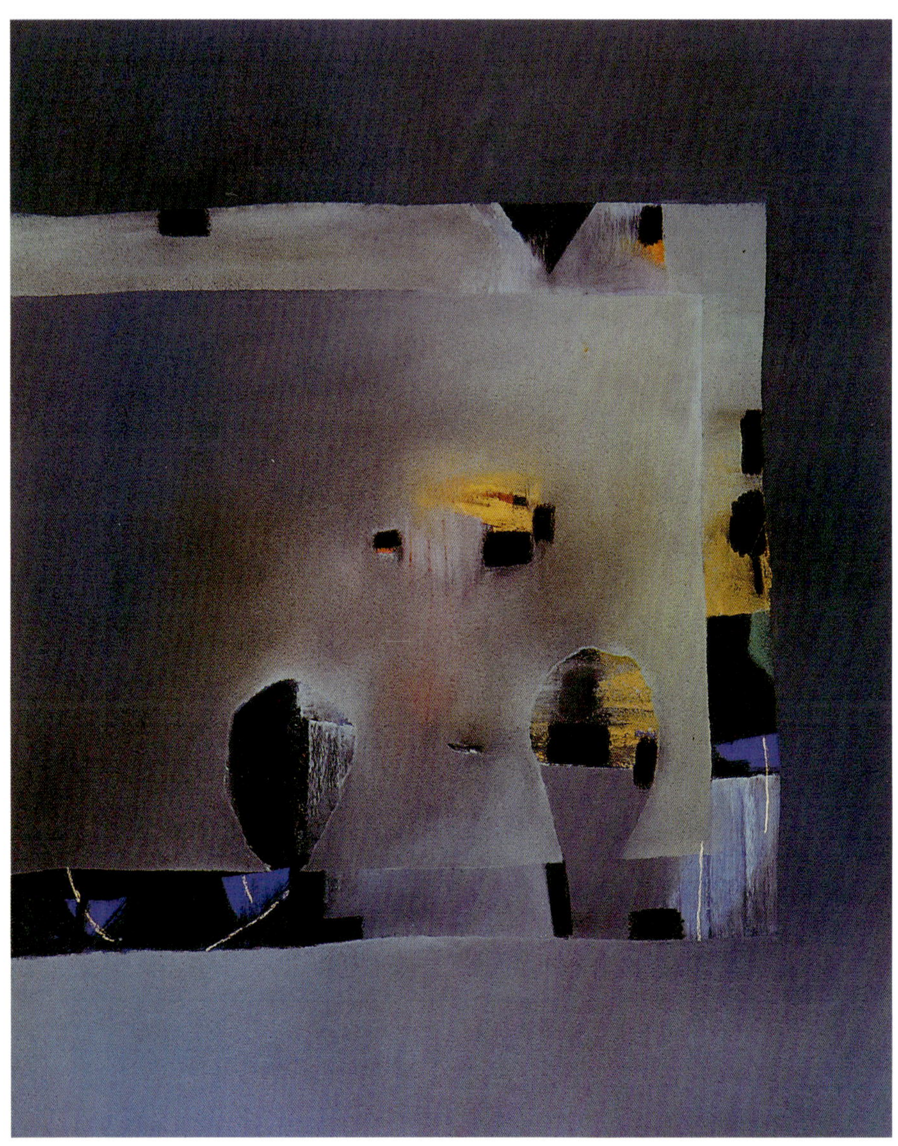

Two Stones and Sunburst, 1994
Pastel
24 3/4" × 20"

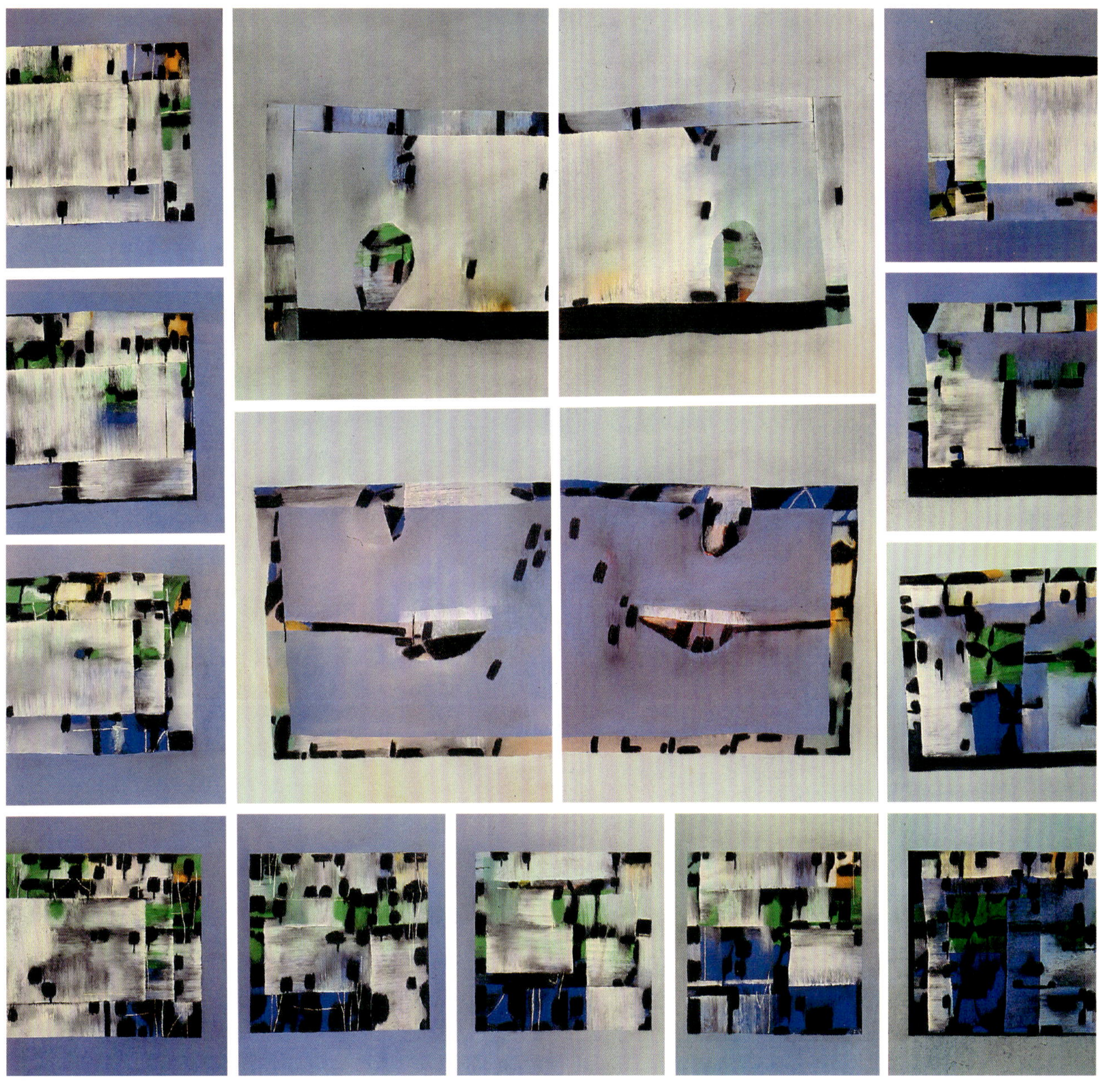

Landscape Vision No. 13, 1993
Pastel
65" × 70"

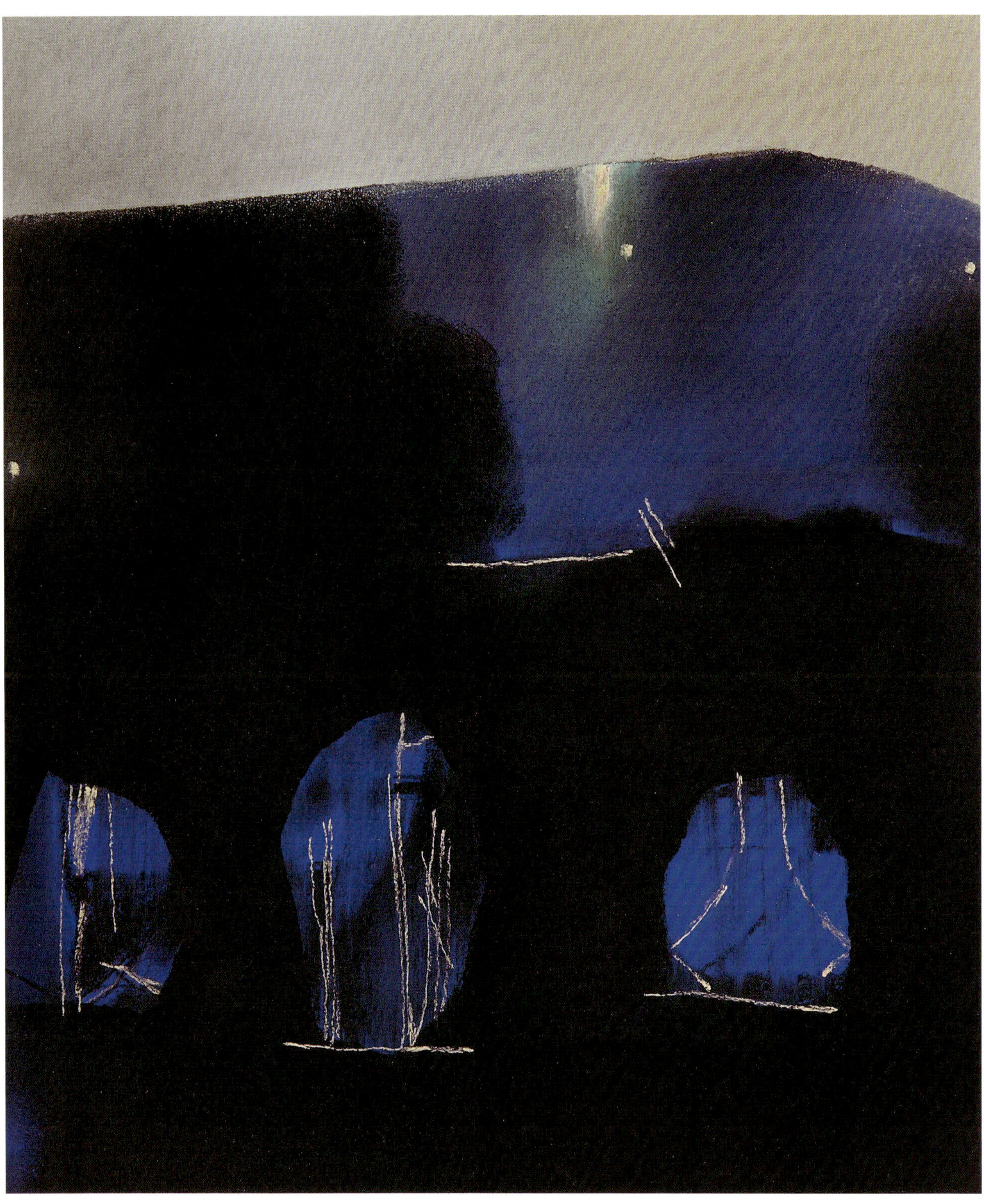

Three Stones, 1993
Pastel
16" × 14$^{1}/_{2}$"
Private Collection

Biographical Notes

1939	Born 22 June, Huddersfield, son of Wilfrid and Nora Blackburn
1955	Wins scholarship to Huddersfield School of Art
1959–62	Royal College of Art, London
1962	Meets Gerhart Frankl and is introduced to pastel
1963	Travels widely in France, Italy and Germany visiting public galleries and private collections
1963–6	Visits Australia where he is employed as part-time Lecturer at the Royal Melbourne Institute of Technology. Travels in Western Australia. Experiments with printmaking 1965–6
1966	Completes *Creation* series. Returns to England, Lecturer, School of Architecture, University of Manchester. Commences work on the *Metamorphoses* series
1970	Commences to exhibit at Agnews in London. Retrospective exhibition at Mappin Art Gallery, Sheffield
1971	Visiting Lecturer, Department of Architecture, University of Melbourne. Visits Central Australia
1973–4	Visiting Associate, Department of Fine Arts, University of Melbourne
1974	Exhibits at Agnews his *Central Australian drawings: studies from Ayers Rock, the Olgas and Nullarbor Desert*. Visiting Fellow, Merton College, Oxford
1977	Visiting Associate, Humanities Research Centre, Australian National University, Canberra
1977–8	Visiting Artist, University of Melbourne
1978	Retrospective at Heslington Hall, Unlversity of York. Travels regularly between England, Australia and the United States
1981	Visiting Professor, Georgetown University, Washington D.C. Begins American 'architectural' drawings and Californian 'beach' scenes
1984	First New York exhibition: Vorpal Gallery. Drawings purchased for Phillips Collection, Washington D.C.
1986	Retrospective exhibition, Dulwich Picture Gallery, London. Begins *Landscape Vision* series
1987	Travels in Canada
1989	Major retrospective exhibition, Yale Center for British Art, New Haven. BBC *Northern Lights* programme. ITV *Celebrations* (30 minute documentary). Commences association with the Hart Gallery
1991	ITV *Artists' Lives* programme. Featured on BBC radio *Kaleidoscope*
1991–4	Working in the North of England

Solo Exhibitions

1965 Argus Gallery, Melbourne
Watters Gallery, Sydney

1967 University of Bradford
Watters Gallery, Sydney

1968 Oldham Art Gallery
University of Leeds
House of Commons, Westminster
Watters Gallery, Sydney

1969 Hatton Gallery, Newcastle upon Tyne

1970 Bradford Festival
University of Swansea
Agnews, London
Retrospective exhibition, Mappin Art Gallery, Sheffield

1972 Agnews, London

1973 Joseph Brown Gallery, Melbourne

1974 Agnews, London

1977 Gallery Huntly, Canberra

1978 Retrospective exhibition, Heslington Hall, York

1979 Retrospective exhibition, Huddersfield Art Gallery

1980 David Jones Art Gallery, Sydney
Solander Gallery, Canberra

1982 International Monetary Fund, Washington D.C.

1984 Vorpal Gallery, New York
Agnews, London

1985 Vorpal Gallery, San Francisco
Royal Institute of British Architects, London

1986 Retrospective exhibition, Dulwich Picture Gallery, London

1989 Yale Center for British Art, New Haven
Hart Gallery, Nottingham
Goldmark Gallery, Uppingham

1991 Hart Gallery, Nottingham

1993 Hart Gallery, Nottingham

1994 Stein Bartlow Gallery, Chicago
Hart Gallery, London
Retrospective exhibition, Huddersfield Art Gallery and tour including Kreis Unna, Germany and Besançon, France

Selected Group Exhibitions

1967 Voightlaender Gallery, Frankfurt

1968 New Art Centre, London

1971 *100 Years of British Drawing*, Agnews, London

1972 *Three Modern British Painters from Agnews, London*
David Jones Art Gallery, Sydney

1973 Galerie d'Arte Moderne, Florence
Art in Yorkshire 1900-1973, Harrogate Festival
Art in Australia 1900-1973, Joseph Brown Gallery, Melbourne

1976 *Australian Art 1876-1976*, Gallery Huntly, Canberra

1977 Oxford Gallery, Oxford

1983 *Drawing International*, Quadrum Gallery, Boston

1987 Fogg Museum, Harvard University, Cambridge, MA

1989 *25 Years* Watters Gallery Sydney

1991 International Art Fair, Olympia, London

1992 *Art '92* Islington, London
Edinburgh Contemporary Art Fair

1993 *Art '93* Islington, London
The Manchester Fine Art Fair
Chicago International Art Exposition
Bath Contemporary Art Fair
Art L.A. Los Angeles International Art Fair

1994 *Art '94* Islington, London
Twentieth Century British Art Fair, London

Public and Corporate Collections

Albertina, Vienna

Art Gallery of South Australia

Art Gallery of Western Australia

Ashmolean Museum, Oxford

Australian National University Art Collection

British Council, London

Contemporary Art Society, London

Fogg Museum, Harvard University

General Electric Company Art Collection

Hatton Gallery, Newcastle upon Tyne

Huddersfield Art Gallery

Leeds City Art Gallery

Mercer Gallery, Harrogate

Museum of Modern Art, New York

National Gallery of Victoria

Phillips Collection, Washington D.C.

Queensland Art Gallery

Sheffield Art Gallery

University of Melbourne Art Collection

University of Prague Art Collection

Yale Center for British Art, New Haven

Yorkshire Arts Association

Selected Bibliography

M.G. McNay, David Blackburn, University of Bradford, *Guardian*, January 1967 (exhibition review)

F.W. Fenton, The Creation in chalk drawings, University of Leeds, *Daily Telegraph*, May 1968 (exhibition review)

Ron Phillips, *The Metamorphoses Drawings*, catalogue essay, Hatton Gallery, Newcastle 1969

Humphrey Brooke, Originality in Pastel, Agnews, *Yorkshire Post*, December 1970 (exhibition review)

Judith Hague, *David Blackburn, Retrospective*, catalogue essay, Mappin Art Gallery, Sheffield, 1970

W.T. Oliver, *David Blackburn Australian Landscapes*, catalogue essay, Agnews, London, 1972

Patrick McCaughey, *David Blackburn*, catalogue essay, Joseph Brown Gallery, Melbourne, 1973

Julian Agnew, *Recent Pastel Drawings by David Blackburn*, catalogue essay, Agnews, London, 1974

Patrick Hutchings, *David Blackburn*, catalogue essay, Gallery Huntly, Canberra, 1977

Sasha Grishin, Landscape as form of diary, *Canberra Times*, 4 October 1977 (exhibition review)

Mario Amaya, David Blackburn, Agnews, *Studio International*, September 1984

Sally Ann Schilling, "Painting In Pastel—3: David Blackburn", *The Artist*, May 1986, pp. 10–13

John Sheeran, *David Blackburn*, catalogue essay, Dulwich Picture Gallery, London 1986

Sasha Grishin, "A Master of Metamorphoses," *Craft-Arts International*, vol. 12, Sydney, May–June 1988 pp. 47–50

Peter Fuller, *David Blackburn: Light and Landscape*, catalogue essay, Yale Center for British Art, New Haven, 1989 (reprinted 1993 in Peter Fuller's *Modern Painters* edited by John MacDonald)

William Zimmer, Exhibition review, *The New York Times*, 1989

John Hart, *The landscape drawings of David Blackburn*, catalogue essay, Hart Gallery, 1989

Sister Wendy Beckett, *David Blackburn*, catalogue essay, Hart Gallery, 1991

Glyn Hughes, *David Blackburn*, catalogue essay, Hart Gallery, 1991

R.S. Phillips, "Light and landscape: An interview with David Blackburn", catalogue essay, Hart Gallery, 1993

Malcolm Yorke, "David Blackburn: Visions and variations", *Contemporary Art*, vol. 1, No. 4, 1993, pp. 30–33